Sovereignty

Other books in the Key Concepts Series

Barbara Adam, Time
Alan Aldridge, Consumption
Alan Aldridge, The Market
Colin Barnes and Geoff Mercer, Disability
Darin Barney, The Network Society
Mildred Blaxter, Health
Harriet Bradley, Gender
Harry Brighouse, Justice
Steve Bruce, Fundamentalism
Margaret Canovan, The People
Alejandro Colás, Empire
Anthony Elliott, Concepts of the Self
Steve Fenton, Ethnicity
Katrin Flikschuh, Freedom
Michael Freeman, Human Rights
Russell Hardin, Trust
Fred Inglis, Culture
Jennifer Jackson Preece, Minority Rights
Robert H. Jackson, Sovereignty
Paul Kelly, Liberalism
Anne Mette Kjær, Governance
Ruth Lister, Poverty
Jon Mandle, Global Justice
Judith Phillips, Care
Michael Saward, Democracy
John Scott, Power
Anthony D. Smith, Nationalism
Stuart White, Equality

Sovereignty

Evolution of an Idea

Robert Jackson

polity

First published in 2007 by Polity Press

Polity Press
65 Bridge Street
Cambridge CB2 1UR, UK.

Polity Press
350 Main Street
Malden, MA 02148, USA

ISBN-13: 978-07456-2338-2
ISBN-13: 978-07456-2337-5 (pb)

A catalogue record for this book is available from the British Library.

Typeset in 10.5 on 12 pt Sabon
by SNP Best-set Typesetter Ltd., Hong Kong
Printed and bound in Great Britain
by MPG Books Ltd, Bodmin, Cornwall

The publisher has used its best endeavours to ensure that the URLs for external websites referred to in this book are correct and active at the time of going to press. However, the publisher has no responsibility for the websites and can make no guarantee that a site will remain live or that the content is or will remain appropriate.

Every effort has been made to trace all copyright holders, but if any have been inadvertently overlooked the publishers will be pleased to include any necessary credits in any subsequent reprint or edition.

For further information on Polity, visit our website: www.polity.co.uk

For Ben

Contents

Preface ix

1 Sovereignty and Modernity 1

 Manifestations of sovereignty 1
 Sovereignty and modernity 5
 Independence and supremacy 10
 Power, authority, responsibility 14
 The discourse of sovereignty 19

2 'A Shocking Idea' 24

 Europe before sovereignty 24
 Respublica Christiana 33
 The revolution of sovereignty 38

3 Sovereigns of Europe and the World 49

 The great transformation 49
 The divine right of kings 56
 Dynastic sovereignty 61
 Western empires 66
 Imperial sovereignty 72

4 Popular Sovereignty 78

 In the name of the people 78
 Parliamentary sovereignty 83

Democratic sovereignty 87
Totalitarian sovereignty 93
National self-determination 97
Territorial sovereignty 104
The end of sovereignty? 112

5 Sovereignty and Humanity 114

Protecting human rights 114
Humanity discourse 115
Human rights, human wrongs, and sovereign
states 120
Human rights under international law 123
Humanitarian intervention 128

6 Sovereignty and Globalization 135

9/11 and the state 135
The globalization thesis 138
The sovereign states system 144
Presuppositions of a states system 150
Between past and future 159

Notes 162

References 164

Index 173

Preface

Sovereignty is an idea of authority embodied in those bordered territorial organizations we refer to as 'states' or 'nations' and expressed in their various relations and activities, both domestic and foreign.[1] In the early twenty-first century there are almost two hundred of those organizations around the world, each one responsible for the territory under its jurisdiction and the people who live there. Sovereignty is at the centre of the political arrangements and legal practices of the modern world. The idea originated in the controversies and wars, religious and political, of sixteenth- and seventeenth-century Europe. It has existed without interruption and spread around the world since that time, and it continues to evolve. The following chapters present a brief but comprehensive account of the idea.

State sovereignty is a fundamental idea of authority of the modern era, arguably the most fundamental. It stands in marked contrast to ideas of authority of other eras, particularly the preceding medieval period of European history, which revolved around the theocratic and transnational idea of Latin Christendom. Sovereignty also stands in marked contrast to ideas of authority in other parts of the world before Western imperial states intervened and established themselves as a global, and no longer merely a European or Western, system of authority. That worldwide episode was only completed in the nineteenth and twentieth centuries.

Prior to European and American intrusion the non-Western world operated with markedly different ideas of authority. Over the centuries the arrangements and practices of sovereign statehood became established in every continent, although not everywhere at the same time or with the same degree of effectiveness or acceptance.

Today sovereignty is a global system of authority. It extends across all the religions, civilizations, languages, cultures, ethnic and racial groupings, and other communities and collectivities into which humanity is divided. The sovereign states system is the only global system of authority that has ever existed. It was once possible for many people, indeed millions, to live outside the jurisdiction of sovereign states. That is no longer possible. There is no inhabited territory anywhere on the planet that is outside. The entire population of the world, more than 6 billion people, find themselves living inside a sovereign state. They may have some choice in determining in which particular state they will live. They have no choice except to live in one state or another, having to make the best of it, enjoying its advantages and opportunities and suffering its hazards and liabilities. The weight of that now universal fact of human affairs is not always fully appreciated.

Sovereignty is a foundational idea of politics and law that can only be properly understood as, at one and the same time, both an idea of *supreme* authority in the state, and an idea of political and legal *independence* of geographically separate states. These two facets of state sovereignty are not separate ideas. They are different aspects of one overall idea. Sovereignty is a constitutional idea of the rights and duties of the governments and the citizens or subjects of particular states. It is also an international idea of multiple states in relation to each other, each one occupying its own territory and having foreign relations and dealings with others, including peaceful and cooperative relations as well as discordant relations and periodical wars.

The core meanings of 'sovereignty' are captured in ordinary English usage as recorded authoritatively in the *Oxford English Dictionary Online* (*OED*), by far the most important dictionary in the language. That source has a vital role in this study because it sets out the historical evolution of the word from its earliest recorded usage by English writers (and by implication English speakers) in the late-medieval and early-modern periods. The history of the word is an integral part of the history of the idea. That deserves emphasis because the word 'sovereignty' nowadays is given many different and often contradictory meanings that are not disciplined by that historical usage. Instead, they are dictated by the theories, methodologies, or ideologies of contemporary commentators on the subject. ' "When I use a word," Humpty Dumpty said, in a rather scornful tone, "it means just what I choose it to mean, neither more nor less" ' (Carroll 1991: ch. 6). That stipulative approach to terminology is particularly noticeable at the present time among social scientists. In their innovative definitions the word 'sovereignty' is uprooted from its historical moorings in ordinary English and made a prisoner of the author's concepts, thereby becoming part of an esoteric jargon, usually to the detriment of our historical knowledge of the subject.

Sovereignty is not originally or primarily an abstract idea fashioned by philosophers and other theoreticians and then applied in practice. It is an expedient idea worked out by kings and other rulers, and their representatives and agents, in response to the novel circumstances of sixteenth- and seventeenth-century Europe. The political arrangements and legal practices of sovereignty came first, the academic theories later. The rulers of early modern Europe initially came up with the idea in their repudiation of the overarching authority of the pope, who was then theocratic head of Latin Christendom. Their successful assertion of sovereignty was a way of escape from papal authority, an act of secession. They also asserted their sovereign authority in relation to rival authorities within their claimed jurisdictions and in relation to their subjects. They employed the idea in their dealings and struggles with each other, including their wars, which led to early formulations of international law. Our classical theories of sovereignty were initially fashioned to understand those expedient arrangements and practices in a comprehensive and systematic way. That classical approach is followed in this study.

The idea of sovereignty is a big idea. It defies academic attempts to pin it down and fit it into tidy analytical categories. When we think we have managed that feat we discover another angle or dimension of the subject that we have not considered. That research experience happened repeatedly in the course of this inquiry, which could have gone on indefinitely but had to end at some point. This book is that point. Sovereign statehood is a multifaceted and wide-ranging idea which calls for an interdisciplinary inquiry. It is impossible to squeeze the subject into any single academic pigeon-hole, such as history or legal studies or political science. None of these disciplines, by themselves, capture the various facets of the idea and stages of its evolution: the political and the legal, the domestic and the international, the present, past, and conceivable future.

The interdisciplinary inquiries upon which this study is based would have been far more difficult to carry out were it not for the existence of the JSTOR and Project Muse digital archives of scholarly journals. Those electronic sources made me more aware of the many journals that deal with sovereignty and made their contents far more readily accessible. *Political Studies; International Affairs; American Journal of International Law; Journal of the History of Ideas; Past and Present; Journal of the American Academy of Religion;* and *Church History* are among the most important of them. In many cases they also quickly led me to books I had not previously known about. The various disciplines that are involved in the study of sovereignty become more fully apparent. That reinforced my conviction that only by adopting an interdisciplinary approach could one hope to come to grips with the subject.

In writing this book I incurred debts to institutions and individuals which I wish to acknowledge. I would like to express my gratitude to the Social Science and Humanities Research Council of Canada which funded some of my early research on the subject. I also thank the Department of International Relations at Boston University for its support of my continuing research. The inquiries for chapter 6 were funded by the Danish Social Science Research Council in cooperation with the Department of Political Science at Aarhus University. I wish to thank my friend and colleague Georg Sørensen for making that possible. An earlier version of chapter 5 was published in Ronald Tinnevelt and Gert Verschraegen (eds),

Between Cosmopolitan Ideals and State Sovereignty (Palgrave Publishers). Chapter 6 is a revised version of an article that appeared in a special issue of *Political Studies* edited by J. M. Hobson (Blackwell Publishers). I am grateful for permission to reprint those refashioned essays here.

The subjects that scholars study sometimes hint at their autobiographies. I was born and have lived for extended periods in Canada, a country that is unsure of its national identity, particularly as regards Quebec, many of whose residents have called for the province's independence. In describing themselves as 'sovereigntists' they even contributed a new word to the English language. The early part of my academic career was spent in Kenya, shortly after that country's independence, which involved a transfer of sovereignty from Britain. I have lived, on and off, in the United States, the cradle of popular sovereignty as registered in the 'Declaration of Independence' and the doctrine of civil rights. That nation also withstood a huge civil war waged over the Confederate States of America's act of secession based on their asserted right of sovereignty. I have regularly visited Britain over the years and watched the government's efforts to suppress the terrorist militias of Northern Ireland, particularly the republican irredentists whose aim was to oblige the British government to relinquish sovereignty over the territory leaving it free to become part of the Republic of Ireland. I have also noticed misgivings of many Britons concerning the European Union's acquisition of authority in certain areas affecting their lives which they believe ought to be exclusively in the hands of the British government. Some of those same concerns are also evident in Denmark, where I have spent happy summers visiting the University of Aarhus.

The preoccupations of academics are bound to affect their families. I would like to thank my wife Margaret for lovingly putting up with her intellectually distracted husband as he struggled to come to grips with the complicated, frequently frustrating, but always fascinating subject of this study. The excellent wine cheerfully dispensed by my son-in-law, Steven Preece, helped relieve the pressure involved in bringing this book to a conclusion. I also want to register a fond debt of gratitude to my daughter, Jennifer Jackson Preece, author of an earlier volume in this Polity series that set an example for my own contribution. I dedicate this book to my grandson, Benedict Jackson-Preece, and to all children in the hope they may grow to adulthood under conditions of security, freedom, and dignity in whatever sovereign state they are bound to live.

R.J.
Boston

1
Sovereignty and Modernity

Manifestations of sovereignty

Sovereignty is one of the constituent ideas of the post-medieval world: it conveys a distinctive configuration of politics and law that sets the modern era apart from previous eras. A. P. d'Entrèves (1970: 67) puts the point well: 'The importance of the doctrine of sovereignty can hardly be overrated. It was a formidable tool in the hands of lawyers and politicians, and a decisive factor in the making of modern Europe.' And not only Europe: sovereignty is a foundation idea of politics and law around the world. By 'sovereignty' I am of course referring to state sovereignty unless otherwise indicated.

This book is written in the genre of the history of ideas. The idea of sovereignty was expediently arranged in the sixteenth and seventeenth centuries by European rulers in the course of their rivalries and struggles, religious and secular. Political and legal thinkers captured the idea, its *modus operandi* and its underlying principles, in commentaries on the subject. Those commentaries are interdisciplinary: the idea is at the heart of political and legal theory, diplomatic as well as religious history, constitutional law and international law. Sovereignty has proved to be remarkably long-lasting. But it is not fixed and unchanging. On the contrary, it has evolved and taken on different personas over time: it has been reformulated periodically to fit the demands and exigencies of specific historical periods or episodes (Philpott 2001). It has never changed fundamentally, however, or out of all recognition. Sovereignty in the twentieth and twenty-first centuries is still recognizably the same basic idea that it was in the sixteenth and seventeenth centuries.

Sovereignty is an arrangement of authority that has important consequences for the millions and now billions of ordinary people, past and present, who have been subjected to it and affected by it. To open our minds to that evolving idea, and to begin to see how it operates, we should contemplate the encapsulated historical events listed below. They illustrate just some of the many and various ways in which sovereignty has been entangled with the modern world across a lengthy span of time, starting in the sixteenth century and continuing into the present century.

- In 1534 King Henry VIII of England demanded and obtained from parliament an Act of Supremacy which gave the king and his successors supreme headship of the Church of England, and immunity from 'foreign law' and 'foreign authorities', particularly the laws and authority of the head of Latin Christendom, the pope.
- In 1649 King Charles I of England was tried by parliament and executed for the crime of erecting 'an unlimited and tyrannical power to rule according to his Will, and to overthrow the Rights and Liberties of the People'.
- In 1662 a quarrel between King Louis XIV of France and Pope Alexander VII, which involved a fracas between the papal guards and the French ambassador, was resolved in 1664 by the humiliating capitulation of the pope, who sent a legate to Paris to express his regret for offending the king's dignity and honour.
- In 1763 at the Peace of Paris, following the end of the Seven Years War in which Great Britain defeated France, the conquered French colony of Quebec was recognized to be part of British North America.
- In 1776 the American Declaration of Independence claimed 'That these United Colonies are, and of Right ought to be Free and Independent States, that they are Absolved from all Allegiance to the British Crown, and that all political

connection between them and the State of Great Britain, is and ought to be totally dissolved; and that as Free and Independent States, they have full Power to levy War, conclude Peace, contract Alliances, establish Commerce, and to do all other Acts and Things which Independent States may of right do.'

- In 1860 and 1861 thirteen southern and slave-holding states of the United States asserted their individual sovereignty, declared their separate secessions from the United States of America, and formed the Confederate States of America (South Carolina, Mississippi, Florida, Alabama, Georgia, Louisiana, Texas, Virginia, Arkansas, North Carolina, Tennessee, Missouri, and Kentucky). Their secession ended with the defeat of the Confederate forces by the Union Army in 1865.

- In 1885 the Signatory Powers of the General Act of the Berlin Conference (Great Britain, Austria-Hungary, France; Germany, Russia, the USA, and several smaller powers) recognized 'the obligation to insure the establishment of authority in the regions occupied by them on the coasts of the African Continent'. Colonization of almost the entire African continent by Britain, France, and other European powers proceeded to take place.

- In a 1918 speech delivered to a joint session of the United States Congress President Woodrow Wilson declared: 'What we demand in this war ... is that the world be made fit and safe to live in; and particularly that it be made safe for every peace-loving nation which, like our own, wishes to live its own life, determine its own institutions, be assured of justice and fair dealing by the other peoples of the world as against force and selfish aggression.' He called for 'a general association of nations ... formed under specific covenants for the purpose of affording mutual guarantees of political independence and territorial integrity to great and small states alike.' That was a major purpose of the League of Nations which Wilson was instrumental in creating.

- In 1941 US President Franklin Delano Roosevelt and British Prime Minister Winston Churchill met on board a British battleship anchored off the coast of Newfoundland and signed the Atlantic Charter, which declared the 'common principles' to which they subscribed, namely 'the right of all peoples to choose the form of government under which they will live', their 'wish to see sovereign rights and self-government restored to those who have been forcibly deprived of them', and their 'hope to see established a peace which will afford to all nations the means of dwelling in safety within their own boundaries'.

- In 1947 the territory of British India was partitioned into two separate and independent states, India and Pakistan. Among the major consequences was the creation of 15 million refugees who now found themselves living on the wrong side of the newly drawn international borders between the two countries, and the outbreak of recurrent wars between India and Pakistan to change those same borders in contested regions, particularly Kashmir.

- In 1960 British Prime Minister Harold Macmillan delivered a speech to the South African Parliament in which he declared that a 'wind of change' was sweeping over the African continent which would result in its complete decolonization: 'Ever since the break up of the Roman empire one of the constant facts of political life in Europe has been the emergence of independent nations . . . In the twentieth century . . . the processes which gave birth to the nation states of Europe have been repeated all over the world . . . Today the same thing is happening in Africa.'

- In 1990 Iraq invaded, occupied, and annexed the neighbouring country of Kuwait, and a successful war against that act of aggression was subsequently fought by the United States, Britain, France, Saudi Arabia, and other countries, with United Nations authorization, to expel the illegally occupying Iraqi army and to restore the sovereign government of Kuwait.

- In 1991 the Soviet Union was dissolved into fifteen new or reconstituted independent states: Estonia, Latvia, Lithuania, Russia, Ukraine, Belarus, Moldova, Georgia, Azerbaijan, Armenia, Kazakhstan, Uzbekistan, Turkmenistan, Tajikistan, and Kyrgyzstan.

- In 1991–2 the Socialist Federal Republic of Yugoslavia disintegrated into wars which resulted in the independence of Serbia-Montenegro, Croatia, Slovenia, Bosnia-Herzegovina, and Macedonia. In 2006 Montenegro separated from Serbia to become yet another independent state of former Yugoslavia.

- In 1993 a 'velvet divorce' was arranged by Czech and Slovak national leaders which resulted in the division of Czechoslovakia into two independent states: the Czech Republic and Slovakia.
- In 1995 a referendum in the Canadian province of Quebec on the question 'Do you agree that Quebec should become sovereign after having made a formal offer to Canada for a new economic and political partnership . . . Yes or No?' The 'no' votes were 51% and the 'yes' votes 49%.
- In 2005 a referendum in France and another in the Netherlands, on a proposed 'Constitution-Treaty' for the European Union, were each defeated.

These episodes, and many others that one could mention, differ in important respects but they all turn, in one way or another, on the idea of sovereignty. It would be difficult, if not impossible, to grasp their historical meaning and significance without that idea. Any discerning reader can see the issues at stake in these episodes without knowing a great deal about them. That is owing to the fact that sovereignty is part of our common-sense understanding of politics and law, although we may not always be fully aware of that. The aim of this study is to sharpen and deepen our knowledge of the idea, so that we can more precisely see how sovereignty operates and the ways it is involved in our lives. This chapter lays out the basic elements and *modus operandi* of the notion. Subsequent chapters narrate phases of its history, including some of the episodes noted above, which are particularly important for conveying the vitality of the idea and its resilience in the face of recurrent and often profound historical change.

Sovereignty and modernity

Sovereignty is a distinctive configuration of state authority. By 'state' I refer to the conventional meaning: a defined and delimited territory, with a permanent population, under the authority of a government. A 'state' could be a colonial state in an empire or a 'state' of the United States. Neither of those states, however, are 'sovereign' states. Governmental supremacy and independence is that distinctive configuration of state authority that we refer to as 'sovereignty'. It is vested in the highest offices and institutions of states as defined by constitutional law: kings, presidents, parliaments, supreme courts, etc. It is also vested in the independence of states: their political and legal insulation from foreign governments as acknowledged by international law. When the government of a state is said to be sovereign, it holds supreme authority domestically and independent authority internationally, at one and the same time.

Sovereignty is a historical innovation of certain European political and religious actors who were seeking to escape from their subjection to the papal and imperial authorities of medieval Europe and to establish their independence of all other authorities, including each other. It is a post-medieval and, indeed, anti-medieval arrangement of governing authority. It is one of the defining markers of the modern world.[1] Charles McIlwain (1932: 392) concluded his seminal work on ancient and medieval political ideas with the following observation:

> The full development of the idea of sovereignty belongs to the historian of modern, not of medieval, political thought . . . conducive to a theory of sovereignty, is the idea of nationality, growing gradually into a sentiment of national unity. The complete expression of this sentiment is not to be found before the sixteenth century.

Whether the sentiment arose at that time, and whether sovereignty requires that sentiment or can subsist without it, are questions for later chapters. The novel and radical idea of sovereignty nevertheless was a repudiation of the European Middle Ages, which rested on the contrary idea of universal Christian theocracy in which the nations or states – *regna* – were not sovereign, as that political and legal condition came to be understood. Medieval *regna* were not independent authorities; nor were they superior authorities. They were subordinate to higher authorities – at least in principle if not always in practice. We cannot begin to understand the idea of state sovereignty without knowing something about the pre-existing medieval idea in reaction to which it was initially conceived. That topic is addressed in the next chapter. Sovereignty is a constituent idea of the modern age. Other eras have had distinctive and different arrangements of authority. The medieval world of Latin Christendom operated without a notion of state sovereignty. The Roman Empire also carried on without it. Modern international law, the 'law of nations', is sometimes seen as a descendant of what Roman lawyers termed *jus gentium*, the human law which applies to peoples, as distinguished from *jus civile*, the civil law which applies to citizens or subjects of the Roman state (*civitas*). The *gens* ('nations') Rome dealt with inside the empire were subjects of its imperial authority and were in no way independent. The 'barbarian' tribes Rome encountered outside the empire and beyond its law and jurisdiction were political objects that were kept in their place by Roman military power. They were not under the authority of Rome. When those 'foreign' and 'rude' peoples could no longer be held in check, they penetrated the empire and eventually destroyed it.

The imperial dynasties of China, the Islamic Ottoman Empire (in the Middle East, south-east Europe, and North Africa) and the Mogul Empire (in South Asia) operated with notions of suzerainty and not sovereignty. They strove to hold sway over diverse territories and populations, usually with the aim of extracting tribute. Their *Weltanschauungen*, and also that of Rome, was hierarchical and not horizontal, and they were on top. Pre-colonial populations of North and South America, hinterlands of Asia, Sub-Saharan Africa, and the Pacific Islands knew little or nothing of sovereignty as understood in this study. They were subjected to it by European conquerors and colonists from whom they also got the idea to demand it for themselves: colonialism provoking anti-colonialism based on the doctrine of self-determination.

State sovereignty is the prevailing idea of political and legal authority of the modern era, defined as the span of time from the early sixteenth century to the present. Sovereignty expresses some core ideas of modernity including the fundamentally important notion of independence: *rex est imperator in regno suo* (the king is emperor in his own realm). That

Latin expression could serve as the motto of sovereignty. Sovereignty was originally a way of escape from dictation and direction by outsiders and it remains to this day an institution that prohibits unwarranted foreign interference in the jurisdiction of states. A basic norm of the UN Charter (Article 2) consecrates the doctrine of equal sovereignty, territorial integrity, and non-intervention. Independence of their homelands from foreign authority is what anti-colonial nationalists demanded, and almost always obtained by securing a transfer of sovereignty from an imperial power. It is what secessionists and irredentists continue to call for and sometimes fight for in various countries around the world.

Sovereignty is a pluralistic arrangement of authority: there is not one sovereign state in the world; there are many sovereign states. Their independence is independence in relation to each other. Their supremacy is supremacy over their own subjects or citizens. Sovereignty was initially asserted by kings against medieval popes and emperors, and against rival monarchs and other independence-minded rulers. It was subsequently claimed by parliaments in political contests with monarchs for supreme authority in the state, by absolute rulers and dictators in asserting their will to power against embryonic parliaments, by anti-colonial nationalists in rebellions and wars against foreign imperialists, by constituent 'states' or provinces of federations in seeking to become independent, by federal authorities in asserting their primacy over 'state' or provincial authorities, and by the people in laying claim to state legitimacy and legality – or more precisely by those who claimed to speak in the name of the people.

States whose governments demonstrate sovereign authority, and only those states, have a place on the political map of the world. A world based on state sovereignty is a world of mutually exclusive territorial jurisdictions: a world without overlapping jurisdictions. Territorial sovereignty can be held jointly, as in the case of condominia, such as the Anglo-Egyptian Sudan (1899–1956), but that is uncommon historically. The inclination and direction is toward jurisdictional exclusivity. Sovereignty can be shared or 'pooled', which is how the political and legal authority of the European Union is often characterized. But that is a somewhat misleading notion because the European Union is not a supreme and independent entity, at least not yet. The territorial sovereignty of Germany, France, Britain, Italy, Spain, Poland, and other states that form the EU remains in their possession on most vital questions, such as those of peace and security.

The lines on the political map – international boundaries – mark that political and legal independence of sovereign states from one another. They are the 'no trespassing' or 'keep out' signs of international politics and law. They delineate and differentiate the most basic 'we' and 'they', 'ours' and 'yours' of global political life. On this side of the line is our place, on that side your place. We are neighbours, and neighbours leave each other alone. The doctrine of non-intervention long has been, and still continues to be, keyed to the idea of state independence and territorial integrity. Sovereignty is, so to speak, the international 'real estate' system of the modern world (Mayall 1990: 20). That world is still a world of fences and hedges even though it is also, increasingly, a cosmopolitan and transnational world, as discussed in chapters 5 and 6.

An international boundary between territorially contiguous, sovereign states is the marker of an authority differentiation, and not a power relation. A boundary is not a wall or dyke or other physical barrier, although it may follow or coincide with a lake or river or mountain range: for example, the Pyrenees Mountains between France and Spain. Boundaries may be and often they are backed by armed force, at least to some degree. Yet that, too, is a contingent feature and not an inherent characteristic. Some boundaries are heavily defended: the Maginot line of French fortifications to block invasion by neighbouring Germany is an extreme case. Some are largely undefended: the United States–Canada boundary. Some are relatively open: borders between European Union member states. How defended or undefended, open or closed, they happen to be is determined by the sovereign states involved. But all international boundaries have exactly the same political and legal significance: they mark the territorial limits of sovereign jurisdictions: inside the borders are our affairs, outside are foreign affairs.

Sovereignty has always been jealously possessed by states and persistently pursued by political actors who are not sovereign but desire to hold and exercise sovereignty: revolutionists, nationalists, populists, secessionists, irredentists, among others. Whether the twenty-first century is making way for a postmodern world that goes beyond or gets away from sovereignty, or not, is an issue addressed in the final chapter. There may of course come a time when the institution is abandoned or abolished and the idea forgotten. That is almost inevitably bound to happen if we take a very long view of the future. No human institution lasts forever. If modern history discloses anything about state sovereignty, however, it is its adaptability to new circumstances, and its continuing popularity around the world.

Independence and supremacy

A sovereign state can be defined as an authority that is supreme in relation to all other authorities in the same territorial jurisdiction, and that is independent of all foreign authorities. 'Supremacy' means the highest and final authority from which no further appeal is available. A sovereign is not subordinate to anybody. 'Independent' means constitutionally separate (James 1986) and self-governing. A sovereign is not somebody else's dependency. 'Sovereignty is the authority of the last word' (Barker 1956: 60). Political actors that are sovereign are not answerable to anybody else. Everybody who is subject to their authority is answerable to them. State authorities can have the last word only if they are both supreme and independent. That is what a sovereign state is. A sovereign is the exclusive and ultimate source of the laws of the state and of all other disclosures and acts of state authority. A sovereign government is usually said to be a 'free' government in the sense that it is free from all foreign authority and law except that to which it has consented or otherwise subjected itself: for example, by means of a treaty. If a state's government were in a position of legal subordination to a foreign government, that authority would be the sovereign, and the state would be an American-style 'state', a colony or some other kind of integral unit or dependency of a larger sovereign state.

That is the classical definition of sovereignty that will be employed in this study. That definition can apply to a republic just as readily as a monarchy, to an autocracy as well as a democracy, to an Islamic republic as well as a Christian kingdom. These are different ways of arranging or constituting state authority in a country. They are not different kinds of sovereignty. A sovereign state is not a particular form of constitution, such as a monarchy or republic or democracy. Nor is it a particular style of governance. Sovereignty is a political and legal foundation upon which various sorts of state constitution can be erected, and styles of governance carried on. If states are sovereign, their ruling authority will have the same basic characteristics of supremacy and independency no matter how they are otherwise constituted or governed. Sovereignty is the basic authority assumption, the underlying premise, of modern politics and law. We are thus inquiring into a fundamental idea.

Sovereign states are Janus-faced: they simultaneously face inward at the population of the country, and outward at other countries. Sovereign governments, by their very organization and orientation, are obliged to face in both directions, to frame foreign policies as well as domestic policies in order to carry out their responsibilities. That is because supremacy and independence are not two separate characteristics: they are two facets of one overall characteristic: sovereignty. Facing inward, the sovereign is the supreme authority in the country. There can be only one sovereign within a country – even if its authority is divided constitutionally between two levels of government, as in a federal state. A federal constitution merely specifies where supremacy resides on any specific issue: that is, whether at the federal level or at the 'state' or provincial level of authority.

Facing outward a sovereign is but one among many such authorities around the world. In the outward exercise of their sovereignty states are never in a position of supremacy. They are in a position of independence. If one state's authority were superior in relation to another state, the latter state would not be sovereign, but instead would be a province or colony or some other kind of component or dependent unit of the former state, which might then more accurately be referred to as a federal state or imperial state. All sovereigns, even the most powerful, must come to terms with that pluralistic reality. They do that by various means and measures that derive from their sovereignty. That includes diplomacy, which is a mutually recognized practice of communication, negotiation, and other forms of interaction between representatives and agents of sovereign states. That also includes international law, which consists of the legal rules (mostly customs and treaties) that obtain in the interactions of sovereign states, either bilateral or multilateral. They do that, as well, by means of commercial relationships, transportation arrangements, and related kinds of international organizations and intercourse. They do that, in the final analysis, by means of war, which reflects the fact that there is no supreme authority above independent states for resolving disputes between them.

Sovereignty is one holistic idea with two conceptual facets: like two sides of a ship's hull, inside and outside. The ship of state is sovereign internally: its crew and passengers are subject to the captain's supreme authority. The ship of state is also sovereign externally: its independence is recognized or at least tolerated and not extinguished by other independent ships sailing on the ocean of world politics, each with its own captain, crew, and passengers. Supremacy and independence cannot exist separately. They can only be distinguished analytically. To change the metaphor: they are two sides of the same political and legal coin.

A colonial government might be said to possess internal sovereignty without having external sovereignty. But that ignores the profoundly important political and legal fact that differentiates a colonial government from a sovereign government: its internal authority is not held independently. It is delegated by an imperial government, which has the final word and thus exercises sovereignty over the colony. A colonial government lacks the vital authority to sail independently on the ocean of world politics. The various colonies of European Africa – British, French, Belgian, Portuguese, etc. – had no independent authority or capacity to conduct diplomatic relations, to establish or employ international laws, to carry on commercial relations, or to declare or wage war. That authority and capability resided with the imperial governments in London, Paris, Brussels, Lisbon, etc.

The most essential element of state sovereignty is independence, as the foregoing example makes plain. Without independent jurisdiction there could be no final word, no commanding authority *in* a country. The government would be answerable to an *external* authority. A foreign authority would be the sovereign. Foreign laws and regulations would have the final word. That was the nub of the constitutional problem that confronted the American colonists before their successful revolutionary war and secession from the British Empire in the late eighteenth century. They bridled at what they saw as intrusive laws and policies of the British imperial government in London, declared their independence, and successfully waged war against Britain to prove their point. Not long afterwards, in the early nineteenth century, their example was followed by the Spanish colonists of Latin America.

Exactly the same problem was confronted by the colonized peoples of Asia and Africa almost two hundred years later. Most of those confrontations, indeed virtually all of them, resulted in transfers of sovereignty from imperial authorities to colonial nationalists. European colonies became independent states. In the decades following the Second World War the number of sovereign states sailing on the ocean of world politics multiplied by a factor of three: from about fifty to one hundred and fifty or more. Today there are almost two hundred in existence. In the course of that worldwide episode the entire territory and population of the planet became organized and integrated into one universal system of locally sovereign states. That remarkable globalization of sovereign statehood, which originally was merely a Western European political and legal arrangement, is addressed in chapter 3.

In the absence of state sovereignty the configuration and movement of world affairs would be significantly different and in all likelihood it would be fundamentally different. In a world federation, for example, states might resemble American 'states' which under the American constitution hold sovereignty jointly with the federal government but they do not hold it exclusively by themselves. The claim that each of them did hold sovereignty exclusively was the legal basis of the act of secession made by those states which formed the Confederate States of America (1861–5). If Britain or France or Germany were not sovereign states, they would be different political and legal places. If the European Union became a federation of some sort, maybe they would resemble New

York, Florida, and California. If the EU continues to deepen constitutionally, there may come a time when these three countries – and all the other countries involved in the EU project – will no longer be sovereign in the classical meaning. The European Union might then resemble the United States of America.

Power, authority, responsibility

Sovereignty is a form of authority, and not a kind of power (Oakeshott 1975), but sovereignty can easily be construed and interpreted as irresistible or compelling power. The test or measure of a state's sovereignty could be seen to reside in its capacity to enforce laws and implement policies. Or it could be seen to rest on its capabilities in dealing with foreign rivals and competitors: for example, in military conflicts or economic contests. That is a misleading idea of sovereignty, usually born of the conflation of power and authority, which is not uncommon in some social science studies of the subject (Krasner 1999).

Power and authority are closely related ideas, but their relation is a contingent or conditional relation, with power under the hood or bonnet of the car and authority in the driver's seat. Authority commands, power executes. Authority is a warrant or licence – an authorization – to exercise power: a search warrant, a driver's licence, a passport or visa, etc. Authority is usually defined by offices that people occupy. That is certainly the case with state authority, which is almost always organized into offices occupied by officials. State power is defined by the instrumental means – the power apparatus – under the control of those officials. How skilled and well-equipped they happen to be, how efficiently and effectively they carry out their official responsibilities, is a question of power and not one of authority. Without power, authority may be hollow. But that is not always the case. It depends on whether an authority is obeyed regardless. A London 'bobby' is universally recognizable as a constable or policeman, and usually obeyed, even though he or she is effectively unarmed, except for a small baton they all carry. For most issues or matters of sovereignty, however, an apparatus of power in the possession and under the direction of state authorities is usually necessary to enforce the laws and carry out public policies, both domestic and foreign. State offices give the people who occupy them access to power, which in many sovereign states is very considerable and credible.

Authority is categorical: either/or, yes or no, green light or red light. Either we possess authority or we do not. Authority is a right or liberty or licence to have access to something or to perform an action or carry out a transaction. Either we have a title deed to a parcel of land or not, a licence to drive a car or not, a right to vote or not, a visa to enter a country or not. Authority is marked by a discernible status or standing or position. Either we are in a position of authority or we are not. A man or a woman is married or not, a citizen of France or not, a member of the British House of Commons or not, the President of the United States or not. Using the same normative logic, a country is independent or not. A government likewise is supreme or not.

Power is not categorical; it is relative, a matter of degree, of more or less. Power is capability and capacity, strength or weakness, in regard to the policies and activities a government or any other actor undertakes, and in relation to other actors it is involved with. Any government, including a sovereign government, requires and usually possesses an apparatus of power of some sort to carry out its decisions and policies. I refer to civil administrations, military forces, police and other law enforcement agencies, intelligence agencies and others means of obtaining and employing vital and sometimes secret information, instruments of public communication and means of propaganda, agencies and techniques for calculating and collecting revenue, regulating the national currency, and managing the national economy, records and statistical information about the population, means of educating the population, providing welfare services and health services, and any other utilitarian means of enforcing the law or implementing public policies. That would include personnel, finances, knowledge, technology, organization, facilities, equipment, infrastructure, and so forth.

A government's capability and capacity cannot confer authority upon it. There was a time when sovereign states exercised their military power to conquer territories and colonize populations. That might be construed to indicate that power confers sovereignty. That, however, is not so. Such acts of armed force were not then regarded as unlawful. Sovereign states possessed a mutually recognized right of conquest and colonization. Such expansive rights and liberties of sovereignty have long ceased to be in effect, a normative change that began after the First World War and concluded after the Second World War. That is not to say that acts of aggression ceased. It is to say that when such military actions were taken, they were generally regarded as illegitimate and unlawful. That was precisely Roosevelt's and Churchill's view of the German conquest and occupation of much of Europe in the early 1940s, as registered in the Atlantic Charter.

Following the same reasoning, a decline in the power of a state cannot – by itself – undercut its authority. A government may be sovereign but may not be very powerful. There has always been a wide range of variation in the capability and capacity of sovereign states. Important domestic and international consequences often stem from whether a state is strong or weak, a great power or a minor power, has a capable government or an ineffective government, and so on. Yet all such relative and variable facts of power have no *conceptual* bearing on state sovereignty, which is a question not of power but of freedom from legal subordination to any other authority.

Canada is a sovereign country. Canada is also, however, a far weaker power, both militarily and economically, than its close neighbour, the United States, and that has a significant bearing on the international relations of those two countries. But that very noteworthy power differential does not subtract in the slightest degree from the sovereignty of Canada. Sovereignty is not a matter of degree. As indicated, it is categorical: either/or. Ottawa is not answerable to Washington, which has no legal authority over the territory and resident population of Canada. Power has no bearing on sovereignty as such, but the capability and capacity available to a sovereign government can have a profound effect on what it is able to accomplish, and how it relates to foreign governments. What the United States possesses in spades, in its international relations with Canada, is very considerable presence and influence, which derives from the power discrepancy between the two countries and their immediate proximity. The interests and policies of the United States usually cannot be prudently ignored by Canadian governments.

That contingent and conditional relation of authority and power was already made famously clear in the mid-seventeenth century by the English philosopher Thomas Hobbes (1946: 109). He was careful to distinguish between the 'authorization' of a sovereign government, via a covenant or social contract, and the 'power and strength' conferred on a government formed in that manner. Such authorized governments were equipped with the 'strength and means' 'expedient' for maintaining domestic 'peace' and providing for the 'common defence'. If governments lacked such power he believed their authority would be hollow. 'Covenants' are categorically different than 'swords', but 'covenants, without the sword, are but words, and of no strength to secure a man at all' (Hobbes 1946: 109). The sovereign state is charged with the heavy responsibility of providing security for its people, and to that end it must exclusively possess and wield two swords: the 'sword of justice' against domestic threats and the 'sword of war' against foreign threats (Hobbes 1993: 176–8). Hobbes closely bracketed sovereignty and power, the authoritativeness of states and the capabilities (and capacities) of states, because he recognized the futility and uselessness of sovereignty without power.

Sovereignty presupposes that there are no limits on the authorized exercise of state power at any point within a sovereign's jurisdiction. If there were limits, the source of those limits would be the sovereign. Sovereigns have no superior. They answer to nobody else. In a Boston seminar on Saudi Arabia–United States relations, a Saudi scholar made a point of emphasizing to his American audience that the Saudi monarchy does not explain or justify its policies to the Saudi people. The monarchy answers to nobody, except God. That doctrine is a contemporary version of the 'divine right of kings' theory of sovereignty which was a commonplace of early modern Europe. It will be discussed in chapter 3. United States President Harry Truman placed a famous sign on his desk in the oval office of the White House which declared: 'the buck stops here'. He was taking presidential responsibility for the

United States of America as laid down by the constitution. But Truman was not the sovereign of the United States. He was not a king or an emperor. Truman, like any other President, answered to the people in accordance with the United States Constitution. In the American democracy, at least in theory, it is the people who do not answer to anybody else. The President and the Congress answer to the people.

With power, it is said, comes responsibility. If we are powerless to do or bring about anything, we cannot be accountable or answerable for anything. Responsibility obviously is limited to that which is within our power to do or prevent. State sovereignty has always raised fundamental questions of responsibility concerning the possession and exercise of power. The governments of Canada or Denmark or any other middle or minor power clearly are not responsible for upholding international peace and security, because they do not have the power either to disturb the peace of the world or restore it. The United States and a few other major powers clearly are responsible because they possess that power. That is recognized in the United Nations Charter, which assigns permanent membership of the Security Council to five great powers, on the grounds that they are vital in defending 'international peace and security', which is a fundamental value of the UN. The *Oxford English Dictionary* quotes Alexander Hamilton in *The Federalist*, no. 63: 'responsibility in order to be reasonable must be limited to objects within the power of the responsible party.'

Since most sovereign states confer extensive powers, and a monopoly of military power ('the sword of war') and police power ('the sword of justice'), on their officials, that raises fundamental questions of accountability and answerability. Those questions are difficult and perplexing because of the constitutional fact that sovereignty is supreme authority and thus the court of last resort in a country. The abuse of state power by government officials is usually the worst abuse of power that anyone can contemplate. That is particularly so if the power being abused is the armed forces of the state, because that is the most destructive and devastating power that exists. And that is exactly the kind of power monopoly that is placed in the hands of the officials of sovereign states. Here we encounter the dilemma of power presented by state sovereignty: armed forces and police forces are necessary to carry on sovereign government, but if that power is not wielded responsibly, the adverse consequences can be profound.

Sovereignty offers no way around the problem of power; nor does any other arrangement of authority. All that one can hope for is that those who have access to the state apparatus of power wield it responsibly and prudently. No constitution can guarantee they will. We have arrived at the inherent and insurmountable problem of power in human affairs, to which there is no fully satisfactory solution, constitutional or otherwise. For those who wield power there is a permanent temptation to abuse their power.

The discourse of sovereignty

The discussion has been striving to capture the fundamentals of sovereignty as a constituent idea of the modern world. An important way to approach the topic is via the discourse of sovereignty. Discourse involves both vocabulary and grammar. When I speak of 'discourse' I am not referring to specialized jargons of academic disciplines. Those are technical languages of experts, many of which have a rather short shelf-life. I refer to ordinary language, in our case that of English speakers. Unlike academic jargons, ordinary languages – English, French, Spanish, Russian, German, Chinese, Japanese, Arabic, etc. – have a social existence that is deeply historical. They are living and working languages of human affairs whose survival rates are generally very high. They provide important information for understanding those affairs, including politics and law.

The *Oxford English Dictionary* is a rich deposit of information on political and legal vocabulary, including 'sovereignty' and closely related words. The word 'sovereignty' has not always meant exactly what it means today. The *OED* defines 'sovereignty' as somebody 'who has supremacy or rank above, or authority over, others; a superior; a ruler, governor, lord, or master'. That obviously is a broad concept. The *OED* records that in the medieval era the term 'sovereign' had more diverse usages than it has today. A 'sovereign' then could be 'a husband in relation to his wife', 'a mayor or provost of a town', 'the Superior of a monastery', among other possibilities. These usages reflect the ideologies and social structures of late-medieval Europe, briefly outlined in the next chapter, in which the state is entangled with the church in an overarching structure of theocratic authority, and the public sphere is not sharply differentiated from the private sphere, as it later came to be. The core usage, however, is clearly political: 'The recognized supreme ruler of a people or country under monarchical government; a monarch; a king or queen'. 'Having superior or supreme rank or power . . . holding the position of a ruler or monarch'.

'Sovereignty' understood as the supremacy and independence of a state is clear by the sixteenth century. What is interesting for our purpose is that this usage (without the connotation of monarchy) survived and the others, such as those noted above, passed into history and became archaic. The term 'state' has a similar historical trajectory, at first signifying diverse meanings: 'the governing body of a town or city' (the German word 'stadt', as in Hamburg stadt, still carries that meaning); 'an order or class of persons regarded as part of the body politic', 'the rulers, nobles or great men of a realm; the government'. These meanings date back to the fifteenth and sixteenth centuries. But what we ordinarily mean by 'the state' becomes fully evident by the end of the sixteenth century: 'a body of people occupying a defined territory and organized under a sovereign government': a sovereign state. That shift in usage is an important marker of the political change from medieval to modern. Quentin Skinner (1978: 352) has written in this connection: 'The surest sign that a society has entered into the secure possession of a new concept is that a new vocabulary will be developed, in terms of which the concept can then be publicly articulated and discussed.' That happened to the idea of 'the state'; it also happened to the closely related idea of 'sovereignty'.

'Sovereignty' thus came to be applied, almost exclusively, to the special authority of the state: it became a politicallegal term. The word acquired meanings that are unambiguously characteristic of the modern era: 'supreme domination, authority or rule'; 'a territory under the rule of a sovereign, or existing as an independent state.' 'Sovereignty' became a qualifier of the term 'state', which implies that some states may not be sovereign: colonial states, protected states, states subject to a suzerain power, 'states' of the USA. Sovereignty subsequently takes another turn as regards the source or location of supreme authority in a state. Originally that location is the ruler (and his or her dynasty): the sovereign. Later it is parliament and later still the people or nation. The *OED* quotes J. S. Mill's definition of representative government as capturing a central usage in the modern meaning of the term: 'That form of government in which the sovereignty, or supreme controlling power in the last resort, is vested in the entire aggregate of the community.' In other words: popular sovereignty, as discussed in chapter 4.

This brings us to the grammar of sovereignty. Grammar consists of the basic rules of intelligible sentence structure and syntax: 'the way in which words are put together' to convey information (*Webster* 1967: 894). We do not think about grammar when we speak or write but it is quietly framing our every act of speech and writing nonetheless. Without grammar we could not communicate either verbally or in writing, with any precision or even with much meaning.

There is a 'grammar' or 'syntax' of sovereignty of a sort: it consists of the basic framework by which such authorities relate to each other and to their citizens or subjects. The previous sections have been laying that out. Here I wish to address it explicitly. Sovereignty is a basic framework in the sense that without it public life would have to rest on some other fundamental rules or structure of authority, and would be as different as that authority was different. Just like grammar, sovereignty may not always be explicitly acknowledged and may, like an iceberg, be mostly hidden from view. But it is present even if we fail to notice, and silently frames the conduct of much of modern politics nevertheless. Sovereignty is a premise or working assumption of modern political life: namely that some authorities are supreme, but others are not supreme; that some authorities are independent, but others are not independent. Those which are supreme and independent are the leading authorities of the modern world. What is most important about that is the following: they are the political people who are most likely to be listened to when they speak from their positions of authority: that is, *ex cathedra*. They are also those political people that most other political people want to be heard by, and for exactly the same reason. The sovereigns are the people with the longest tongues and the largest ears.

As anyone who has visited Legoland in southern Denmark knows, Lego constructions can be different and diverse, yet the building blocks are all the same. Sovereignty is like Lego: it is a relatively simple idea but you can build different things with it, large or small, as long as you follow the rules. As indicated, various arrangements of statehood – monarchical, republican, autocratic, democratic, totalitarian, and so forth – have been constructed on sovereign state foundations. Sovereignty can also be employed to do different – sometimes very different – political things. English (later British) rulers used sovereignty to separate themselves from Latin Christendom. Then they used it to build an empire that eventually encircled the globe. Then they used it to decolonize their empire and thereby created a multitude of new, locally sovereign states in Asia, Africa, and elsewhere. Then they turned around and used their sovereignty to become part of the European Union and to participate in its common affairs.

Those various uses of sovereignty, along with others not mentioned, span the time from the early sixteenth century to the present day. Over that lengthy period sovereign players changed, their territorial jurisdictions expanded or contracted, some old jurisdictions were extinguished and some new ones were created, a process of change that has continued to the present era. The locus of sovereignty in many if not most places was relocated from rulers and dynasties to parliaments and estates or social classes, and then to the nation or people as a whole. The uses to which sovereignty was put varied from place to place, and from time to time. Throughout that lengthy period, however, the basic elements remained constant: political life continued to cycle on the linked premises: that the land surface of the planet is partitioned into a number of separate bordered territories, that a certain determinate authority is supreme over all other authorities in each territory, and that those supreme authorities are independent of all foreign authorities. Those premises have remained unchanged down to the present day.

Of special interest to this inquiry is the way in which sovereignty accommodates both continuity and change in political life: it remains the same in some respects but changes in other respects. Sovereignty thus reveals itself as an idea that on the one hand is constant over time, but on the other hand is subject to significant variation in its historical manifestations. What is stable and continuous over the entire history of sovereignty is the idea that a sovereign government is an authority that is supreme over all other authorities in the same territorial jurisdiction, and is independent of all foreign authorities. What are changeable and variable are the answers that have been given to the questions: Who is entitled to hold and exercise sovereignty? What are the uses to which sovereignty can be put? Those changing answers reveal different doctrines or ideologies that prevail in different historical periods and in different places at the same time.

My purpose, then, is to explore the evolving idea of sovereignty in historical outline. Limitations of space dictate that this essay can only be an abridgement of a large subject. The main questions that can and I believe should be asked of sovereignty are the following: What is its character and *modus operandi*? What was involved in the emergence of sovereignty as the central arrangement of authority of the modern world and its extension around the globe? What was involved in its shift of locus from the rulers to the ruled in many places – although not everywhere? What are the sovereign rights of states in relation to the human rights of individual men and women? Is a globalized world possible without state sovereignty? What would be involved in going beyond sovereignty in politics and law? How deeply rooted are the underlying premises of state sovereignty?

2
'A Shocking Idea'

Europe before sovereignty

The modern world of sovereign states cannot be understood in perspective without also understanding the pre-existing world of medieval Europe in which politics and religion were integrated into one overarching theocratic order. Our modern thinking about government flows effortlessly in secular and scientific grooves. Medieval thinking flowed just as effortlessly in religious and theological grooves. Referring to England just before the Protestant Reformation, one historian remarks: 'The truths of religion had so long been presupposed that they rose before the mind as inevitable and enclosing as the sky' (Mathew 1948: 5). If we can understand, even if only in brief outline, what that pre-modern world was like and what the political change from medieval to modern involved we shall be in a better position to assess the evolution of the idea of sovereignty because we shall then appreciate where, when, how it came into historical existence. Perhaps we shall even begin to see why we have sovereignty and why it has been with us, unfolding, but without interruption, changing shape but not its basic substance, for the past three or four hundred years.

We should therefore be mindful that the historical passage from medieval to modern involved issues of religion as much as politics: in the medieval world of Latin Christendom church and state were entangled, almost inextricably. The 'public' discourse of that earlier world was ecclesiastical as well as political. There was no discourse of politics entirely separate from that of religion. That is because religion sanctified all authority, temporal as well as spiritual. The king was in part a religious authority. The pope was in part a political authority. The administration of kingdoms at the highest levels involved cardinals, archbishops, bishops, and other senior clergy. There was not yet any clear idea of 'the state' and much less the nation-state or the sovereignty of the people. That came later. We should also keep in mind that Europeans at that time possessed no clear distinction between the national and the international. That too came later. Those familiar modern ideas were not in the minds of medieval Christians. They conceived of themselves as belonging to one, unified Christian world – Christendom – however loose and wobbly its unity might be in practice.

Christian unity was an age-long hope but not always an accomplished historical fact. There were two Christian empires during the Middle Ages: Latin Christendom in the west centred on Rome, and the Greek Byzantine Empire in the east centred on Constantinople (Istanbul). The Christian authorities of the east did not recognize the supremacy of the pope. Only Latin Christendom – medieval Europe – was displaced, eventually, by the modern sovereign states system. The Byzantine Empire was conquered and destroyed by the Ottoman Turks in the mid-fifteenth century and its territories and populations were incorporated into their Muslim empire. That greatly delayed the emergence of sovereign states in the Ottoman parts of Europe, which did not arrive until the nineteenth and early twentieth centuries.

Medieval Europe consisted of various *regna*: islands of local political authority scattered across the western part of the former Roman Empire. Most *regna* were deposited, haphazardly, in various places during and after the decline and fall of Rome and the settling down of numerous migratory peoples, the so-called barbarian tribes: Visigoths, Huns, Ostrogoths, Sueves, Vandals, Lombards, Franks, Saxons, among others (Bury 1967). The tribal leaders assumed local control in their territories of conquest or occupation – not only control of their own people but also the Romanized and Christianized populations who had long been settled in those territories under the *pax Romana*. The Christian religion, its institutions, and its authorities, including the papacy, survived the fall of the Roman Empire. Christian bishops came to terms with the tribal leaders or their descendants and converted them to Christianity (Fletcher 1998). Particular *regna* eventually came to be identified by the land and its people, which call attention to the germ of nationality they contained: *regnum Anglicana* (England), *regnum Gallicum* (France), etc.

The age of conversion lasted for a very lengthy period, from the fourth to the fourteenth century, during which time the frontier of Latin Christian civilization was pushed gradually but relentlessly ever deeper into the hinterlands of Western, Eastern, and Northern Europe (Fletcher 1998; Bartlett, 1993). It was not until the ninth or tenth centuries that we can speak intelligibly of *respublica Christiana*, the Christian Commonwealth of Europe, as defined below (Morrall 1958: 12–27; Mayr-Harting 1993: 101–30). Converting barbarians to Christianity was conveniently an act of civilizing them too: once they were Christians they could no longer be pagans or heathens or barbarians. Converting rulers also meant converting the people living in the territories they ruled. An outpost of the Christian church, headed by a bishop, was established in the newly inaugurated Christian kingdom. *Regna* and *ecclesia*, a sort of 'state' and church, were two elements of a single theocracy which presided, albeit loosely and with periodic local interruptions, over a gradually expanding area of Europe for a thousand years.

The *regna* were not independent as we understand that idea. Yet neither were they provinces of an overarching imperial state, as in the Roman Empire. They were something in between. *Regna* were the home of *ecclesia* or churches which it was the duty of Christian rulers to protect. These initially missionary outposts later became regional branches of Christendom: *ecclesium Anglicana*, *ecclesium Gallicum*, etc. Protection given to Christianity by the later Roman Empire from the time of Emperor Constantine was now provided, very haphazardly at first, by the new rulers that had destroyed it. Periodically one of those rulers rose to a position of supremacy, such as the Frankish king who was crowned by Pope Leo III in AD 800 as Roman Emperor Charlemagne. The question whether the *ecclesia* that were protected by the *regna* were under their jurisdiction or were under that of the papacy, whether temporal rulers could appoint bishops and abbots, later developed into what is known as the Investiture Contest between several succeeding emperors and their papal antagonists (Morrall 1958: 28–40). Successive popes claimed that as Vicars of Christ that authority resided exclusively in their hands.

Medieval Europe had an overarching, centralized church (*sacerdotium*) headed by the Bishop of Rome, the pope, and there was an emperor of sorts (*regnum*), who was more significant at some times, less at others. This dualist *respublica Christiana* could thus be understood as constituting a theological-political empire. Although far weaker and much less developed, it was a recognizable descendant of the old Roman Empire, which in its later stages had a Christian Emperor, after the conversion of Constantine (Knowles 1967: 5). Christian rulers of *regna* were duty-bound to defend the faith against internal and external enemies and threats. One of the important ways they did that was by protecting bishops and other clergy and their churches, monasteries, abbeys, priories, etc. Another way was by leading Christian crusades to liberate the holy lands of the near east and the territories of the lower Iberian peninsula from the Muslims who then occupied them.

The late-medieval map of Latin Christendom that eventually emerged after many centuries was not a territorial patchwork of different colours, which represent independent countries under sovereign governments whose populations exhibit distinctive national identities. Instead, it was a complicated and confusing intermingling of lines and colours of varying shades and hues. A kind of 'Europe' did of course exist as the territory of a distinctive family of peoples. But its component parts – *regna* – cannot be regarded as sovereign states. 'Europe was not divided up into exclusive sovereignties, but was covered by overlapping and constantly shifting lordships' (Clark 1960: 28). It was unusual for a king's realm to be concentrated and consolidated at one place. A ruler's territory would often resemble an archipelago: peripheral parts were scattered, like islands, among the territory of other rulers; core parts were perforated and interrupted, like lakes, by the intervening jurisdictions of other authorities. Some rulers held fiefdoms within the territorial domains of other rulers, which gave them the status of semi-independent vassals.

In short, many medieval *regna* consisted of heterogeneous populations and often non-contiguous territories. By the later Middle Ages and early-modern period that was a striking feature. Rulers occupied different offices in their different territories, which affected the way they governed them. After 1460, for example, the ruler of Denmark was a hereditary king in Copenhagen and its surrounding lands and seas, but he was only an elected duke in the duchies of Schleswig-Holstein in the lower peninsula of Jutland on the German frontier. The German kings of Prussia were absolute monarchs in Königsberg (Kaliningrad) but in Berlin they were imperial vassals of the Holy Roman Emperor. The Swedish kings were absolute monarchs in Sweden but after the Peace of Westphalia (1648) they were subjects of the Holy Roman Emperor in their newly conquered territories of northern Germany. Even the greatest monarch, the French king, was at one time a vassal of the Holy Roman Emperor in Alsace. The Habsburg emperors themselves, the last medieval imperial dynasty, were autocrats in Vienna and Prague but only constitutional monarchs in Brussels. It was like that across much of Europe in the late Middle Ages.

The *regna* were neither supreme nor independent, neither 'states' nor 'nations' as we understand those terms. It was scarcely possible to speak of 'the state'. There were of course kingdoms and other territorial lordships, large and small. A king or a duke or a municipal government or the head of a religious order could exercise lordship, which was not restricted to dynastic or even to noble families – although most lordships were the hereditary tenures of such families. Kings were intermediate authorities: they were above most other authorities, temporal and spiritual, but they were beneath God and also beneath the pope in certain matters. And much of the time local rulers enjoyed noteworthy insulation from the rule of kings: they were semi-autonomous but they were not fully independent either. 'Lordship' involved 'a proprietary right to territory' (Keen 1991: 262). But it did not entail supremacy and independence.

Kings contested with rival authorities and powers both inside and outside their realms. The first and foremost rival was the Church, including not only the pope and his clerical administrators in Rome but also his representatives (cardinals, archbishops, bishops, etc.) who held senior offices within *ecclesium Anglicana, ecclesium Gallicum*, etc. Some of those clergy were often the most important royal officials in the kingdom. The Church also included religious orders some of which were among the greatest landowners. The second rival was the feudal nobility who were rulers of local fiefdoms and collectively formed a ruling class or caste that was ready to question and sometimes resist the authority of the king. The third rival was the local authorities (*communitates*), particularly cities and their guilds, some of which were semi-independent powers: the medieval City of London is an example. Beyond their realm, kings faced each other. But that quasi-international relation was not as sharply defined as it would become at the end of the Middle Ages and the start of the modern era. Wars were fought against other kings, but wars were also fought against the pope and against powerful nobles. Wars were also fought by medieval knights for whoever they owed military services, and by mercenaries – private armies – for whoever was their paymaster. It was not until the emergence of sovereign states in the sixteenth and seventeenth centuries that war-making authority and war-making power become concentrated and monopolized in the hands of kings, and war became one of the most telling features of their international relations now properly so called.

In the European Middle Ages political life was not sharply differentiated from religious life or family life or economic life or other departments of social existence. Government authority was not unambiguously 'public'; a king ruled the realm as prince but a king also held extensive 'private' estates of which he or she was lord and master. Government was in many places the affair of certain royal families: political dynasties. In other places it was the corporate activities of religious foundations or commercial organizations. In the countryside, where almost everybody lived, the effective authorities were the local lords of the manor, the bishops of the Church, the heads of the monasteries and abbeys, and the parish priests. 'The people' or 'nation' scarcely existed as such. They were a population, often speaking distinctive vernacular languages or dialects, which separated them from each other and also from officials of church and state, who typically spoke Latin. The idea of belonging to a nation-state, the sense of having a national identity, had not yet been implanted in the minds of people. They thought of themselves in quite different ways. They were Christians. They had no other common name for themselves that extended beyond the local community. People took their social standing, or status, from their appointed place in a steep social hierarchy, at the top of which was God and at descending steps on the social ladder were the pope, the emperor, kings, barons, bishops, knights, priests, merchants, craftsmen, parishioners, peasants, serfs.

That arrangement is commonly referred to as feudalism, which had a strong personal element known as vassalage: a contractual relation of patron and client that involved a mutual commitment to protect and to serve. Medieval European society consisted of countless ladders of patron–client ties. Virtually everybody was a vassal of somebody else (Ganshof 1964: 69–105). Some people had more than one master. Royal servants who were clergy had two masters: king and pope. Patron–client ties between king and baron, bishop and priest, lord and knight, master and servant were so strong that the territorial notion of authority was muted – for such ties were personal and not territorial, and they often leap-frogged across geographical boundaries (Bloch 1964: 367). Most ordinary people, the mass of rural peasants, were virtual chattels of land-holders – local nobles, religious foundations (monasteries, abbeys) – far more than they were subjects of monarchs or emperors. In other words, they were serfs – agricultural labourers permanently bound to their lord and master – in a society defined by the institution of serfdom. 'Thus to speak of a feudal "state" is really a misuse of terms; for a feudal organization of society was a substitute for its organization in a state, and a perfectly feudal condition of society would be not merely a weak state, but the negation of the state altogether' (Brierly 1936: 3). By 'state' Brierly means 'sovereign state'. Ernest Barker (1956: 13) comments in the same vein: 'there was an abundance of "Society" in the territorial kingdoms, or "Estates-States", of the Middle Ages; but there was very little "State".'

Some people, usually a very small minority, were 'citizens' (*cives*) in the original meaning of the term as members of a city (*civitas*). Citizenship was the status of certain urban dwellers – merchants, bankers, lawyers, manufacturers, craftsmen, etc. – who controlled guilds and other governing bodies under which civic life was carried on. A medieval *civitas* was a free city, more or less, but it was not an independent nation-state. Most such cities were located in central and southern Germany and northern Italy. Some cities acquired the status of semi-independency by gaining corporate rights from the crown to constitute themselves as a separate political body and to conduct their common affairs with a measure of self-government. They had their own laws. The medieval corporation of London, governed by representatives of guilds, enjoyed a significant degree of self-government. By the high Middle Ages (AD 1200–1500) in northern and central Italy cities such as Venice and Florence were more developed politically and already possessed virtually independent governments: here were the first recognizably modern sovereign states which together formed a regional states system.

A striking impression that the European Middle Ages convey to anyone looking back from our vantage point at the start of the third millennium is that of complexity and confusion concerning legal authority. Marc Bloch (1964: 359) identifies three 'dominant features': extensive 'fragmentation' of judicial authority; 'tangled' and puzzling interconnections of courts and other judicial bodies; and lastly their 'ineffectiveness'. Legal cases could be heard in different courts which exercised parallel and overlapping jurisdiction. That often invited or provoked legal disputation not only by people who brought cases to different courts but also by courts and jurists themselves. If litigants failed to obtain satisfaction in one court they could seek it in another or even be invited to do so. The most significant cause of such conflicts was the coexistence of two parallel bodies of law: canon law and civil law. Canon law was the law of the church, which applied to all Christians – the law of Latin Christendom. Civil law was the law of the realm, which applied to all subjects of the king. But clear lines could not always be drawn between canon law and civil law, between ecclesiastical courts and royal courts. The subjects of both laws were the same group of people: everybody was at one and the same time a member of the church and a subject of the crown. The arrangement was a standing invitation to anyone who might be tempted to exploit it. The possibilities of abuse were considerable.

The administration of *regna* was often in the hands of university-trained clerics who were the most highly educated section of the population. In England at the end of the Middle Ages 'the majority of bishops' were government officials (Mathew 1948: 10). But their dual status could be a source of difficulty and even discord. They could find themselves in a conflict with the pope if they served the king too faithfully, or with the king if they were too devoted to the pope. They performed a perilous act on a high wire one end of which was held by the king and the other end by the pope: failure could bring imprisonment or even death at the hands of the king's executioners, or ex-communication and a sentence of eternal damnation at the command of the pope.

To summarize the discussion thus far: the political world of the Middle Ages was diverse, dislocated, and disjointed – even if it did have some degree of centralization via the subordination of *ecclesia* and *regna*, bishops and kings, to the Catholic hierarchy usually centred on Rome. Ruling authority was tenuous even at the best of times. While there was a layer of authority that we might refer to as 'the state', the royal jurisdictional sphere of the king, there were significant levels of authority both above and below, which contributed to the weakness rather than the strength of kings and kingdoms. Above the king was the political-theological authority of Latin Christendom. Beneath the king were various secular and spiritual authorities, some of which were virtually independent. And at almost the same level as the king were the religious-political magnates: cardinals, archbishops, bishops, etc. who might be in the administrative service of the king but received their religious office from the pope in Rome. Many bishops were rulers of semi-independent territorial lordships – bishoprics – that were scattered across Europe. They were some of the greatest landowners of medieval Europe. Also among the leading authorities and landowners in the countryside were religious orders: Benedictines,

Cistercians, Augustinians, Carthusians, Franciscans, Carmelites, Dominicans, and so forth (Knowles 1979).

We shall not correctly understand the Middle Ages if we suppose that church and state were separate, that the political sphere operated independent of the religious sphere. To think in that way is to fall into a modern habit of thought. Instead of the separation of church and state, and the subordination of church to state, the medieval relation was one of interdependency and involvement of both church and state in the affairs of Latin Christendom at all levels of authority (D'Entrèves 1939: 12). Church and state were sometimes partners, sometimes rivals, in a world that was ambiguously both theological and political at one and the same time.

Respublica Christiana

Medieval Europe was – at the most basic level of human ideas, thought and feeling – a community of Christian believers. It was the sacred duty of the pope and the emperor, of kings, barons, bishops, priests, and indeed of every Christian to uphold and defend that community. The only uniform institution that existed across Western Europe and by far the most important institution of the Middle Ages was the cosmopolitan 'Christian Commonwealth' or *respublica Christiana* built on that community, which was devoted to Christian redemption and salvation. That religious purpose stood above all others in the teleology of the Middle Ages: above prosperity, above freedom, above order, above justice, even above peace – although that goal was next in importance. Garrett Mattingly (1988: 16) observes: 'belief in the actual unity of Christendom, however variously felt and expressed, was a fundamental condition of all medieval political thought and activity.' Even if the actuality of unity could frequently be in doubt and was sometimes non-existent, 'the belief in unity was deep-seated and died hard' (Keen 1991: 12).

Given the fragmentation of medieval Europe, the conception of an overarching authority may seem illusory. It is important to keep in mind, however, that *respublica Christiana* was 'a canon of interpretation' or point of reference for making decisions and judging policies and activities of those with power: 'no doubt the idea of the *respublica Christiana* is simply an approximation; but it is an approximation which is of great help in visualising the main points in which medieval political theorists, even though of very different opinions, are fundamentally at one' (D'Entrèves 1939: 12). *Respublica Christiana* was the way that religious and secular authorities justified their conduct. It was their mental map and their discourse of authority: the theological-political framework in terms of which they thought of themselves and spoke of their world.

If we can stretch a word and speak of 'sovereignty' during the medieval period, in the first instance the sovereign was God, whose commands were acknowledged by Christians as requiring their obedience. In the second instance it was the pope, the Bishop of Rome and Vicar of Christ, God's representative on earth, who presided over Latin Christendom. 'The pope had been entrusted with the two swords, temporal and spiritual . . . he bestowed the use of the former upon the secular ruler, but only so that he might serve the ends of the pope to whom he owed his position as emperor' (Knowles 1967: 10). That came to be known as 'the allegory of the Two Swords' (Gierke 1987: 13), which also applied to leaders of *regna* who had a Christian duty to use the temporal sword to defend the faith. The core idea was the notion that secular authorities no less than spiritual authorities were Christ's subjects and servants. According to St Paul in his epistle to the Romans:

> Let everyone obey the authorities that are over him, for there is no authority except from God . . . It is not without purpose that the ruler carries the sword; he is God's servant, to inflict his avenging wrath upon the wrongdoer. You must obey, then, not only to escape punishment but also for conscience sake. (Romans 13)

Since it was based on doctrines and teachings of the Christian religion there was no room for anyone who questioned Catholic orthodoxy or rejected the authority of the pope. Medieval Christians thus drew a sharp line to separate their world of 'true faith' from the non-Christian world of pagans and barbarians, the heretical world of false Christianity, and the anti-Christian world of Muslims. A similar border of civilization was later drawn to separate the European world of sovereign states – understood as coterminous with the 'civilized' world – from the non-European world – deemed to be uncivilized and therefore unworthy of sovereignty and thus a legitimate candidate for European conquest and colonization.

Within Latin Christendom, as indicated, there were no firm and fixed political borders denoting separate territorial jurisdictions that we would understand as sovereign states. Europe was a cosmopolitan Christian world, a community of Christians, who were subject to overlapping laws and regulations: ecclesiastical (canon) law, civil or common law, the laws of chivalry, civic and municipal regulations, local customs, and so forth. That is evident even in regard to diplomacy, which the modern world identifies specifically as activities and relations of representatives and agents of sovereign states or of international organizations founded and controlled by states: for example, the United Nations. In medieval Europe, however, the most important diplomats were the representatives and agents of the Church. Christian emissaries were concerned with ensuring conformity with the laws and teachings of the Church (*jus ecclesiasticum*) in every part of *respublica Christiana*. They were also charged with the responsibility of promoting the unity, peace, and tranquillity of Christendom.

Peace was at the heart of Christian teleology and teaching: living in accordance with the Christian Gospel. Peace was not merely an arrangement or condition of non-hostilities between rulers. Peace was an active state of affairs, the Christian peace, which all Christians were duty-bound to strive to achieve, especially those who had the power to create peace or disturb the peace: namely rulers and warriors. War could only be waged for a just or holy cause defined in Christian terms. Wars waged among Christian rulers for wholly secular reasons were unlawful and blasphemous. War was always regrettable but it was justifiable if it was in the service of Christ. 'Because of its concern with peace among Christians, the Church elaborated laws of war meant to mitigate the consequences of internal strife in Christendom, to distinguish between just and unjust wars, and to justify intervention against unjust breakers of the peace' (Mattingly 1988: 19–20). Thus, in the final analysis, war among Christians, as we would understand it, was always internal war or civil war, never international war.

The dualistic arrangement of authority that characterized *respublica Christiana* set the stage for contests for supremacy between emperors and popes which dogged and punctuated lengthy periods of medieval history (Figgis 1965: 38–65). Each side claimed for itself the office of God's exclusive representative on earth; for both parties the claim was often crafted via conceptions of the old Roman Empire in which the emperor was both god and man. The Holy Roman emperor could and did claim to hold the office of *sacerdotium* against the pope. And the Bishop of Rome could and did claim that the papacy was a *regnum* superior to that of the emperor. Struggles occurred from time to time, and not only between the pope and the emperor. Parallel conflicts occurred between the leaders of the local churches (e.g. *ecclesium Anglicana*) and the rulers of the *regna* in which they were located (e.g. the Kingdom of England). The local church could become closely identified with a particular kingdom and distanced from Rome. Ernest Barker (1956: 12) notes that in the fourteenth century certain lawyer propagandists of kingship argued that 'each territorial king was the emperor of his kingdom (*rex in regno suo est imperator regni sui*)' which amounted to 'a rebuttal of imperial claims of sovereignty'. That could even become an assertion of ecclesiastical control by monarchs who might demand a big say in church appointments and might even install themselves as head of the church in their kingdom, as eventually happened, for example, in newly Protestant England, Denmark, and Sweden.

These internecine struggles provoked a body of legal and political theory, for or against one side or the other, which began to change the way leading people thought about their world and eventually opened European minds to the idea of a world of sovereign states. Dante Alighieri argued for a universal monarchy to suppress the persistent wars between *regna* and to pacify the world, which he referred to as human civilization (*umana civiltà*). He was an early cosmopolitan thinker. Another Italian, Marsiglio of Padua, also argued for a human-focused political authority but one in which the *regnum* was a separate and paramount arrangement of purely secular authority based on positive law (D'Entrèves 1939: 64; Morrall 1958: 106). Marsiglio thus gives an early intimation of the doctrine of state sovereignty, which during the Renaissance and Reformation was to prove so important in legitimating the authority of secular rulers. He was an early statist thinker. He has been characterized, rather aptly, as 'the first political sociologist of the middle ages' (Morrall 1958: 107).

To sum up thus far: kings and other kinds of territorial rulers in the Middle Ages were partners in a larger theological-political order and they had a duty to defend the Christian faith and to safeguard the Christian peace in their spheres of jurisdiction in accordance with Christian teachings. Henry Bracton, an English medieval lawyer, makes this point: 'The king is below no man, but he is below God and the law; law makes the king; the king is bound to obey the law, though if he breaks it, his punishment must be left to God' (as quoted by Maitland 1979: 100–1). A leading legal historian comments:

> it will be well to remember that our modern theories run counter to the deepest convictions of the Middle Ages – to their whole manner of regarding the relation between church and state . . . it is very necessary for us to remember that the men of the 13th century had no such notion as sovereignty, had not clearly marked off legal as distinct from moral and religious duties, had not therefore conceived that in every state there must be some man or some body of men above all law. (Maitland 1979: 100–1)

In the Middle Ages it would therefore be difficult to ask the question: Who is sovereign in this country? To have argued that there is an authority that is superior to all other authorities in the realm, and is independent from all foreign authorities, including *respublica Christiana*, would be to advocate a scandalous idea, because it would be in contempt of one's most fundamental obligations, which were those of a Christian man or woman that were valid even if the man or the woman were a king or queen (Maitland 1979: 101; Mattingly 1988: 23, 44). Yet that is the major premise of state sovereignty. It was left for King Henry VIII of England,

and some other princely rulers, not only to entertain that idea but to act on it decisively thereby setting a compelling precedent. It was left for Niccolò Machiavelli, Martin Luther, Jean Bodin, and Thomas Hobbes not only to ask such questions (or very similar questions) but also to answer them in ways that disclose a radically new kind of thinking about authority that signalled the end of the Middle Ages and the beginning of the modern era.

The revolution of sovereignty

If we had to summarize in a few words what was in fact a long drawn out, complicated, sometimes contradictory, and often ambiguous but nonetheless fundamental and thoroughgoing change, we could say that the political shift from medieval to modern involved the destruction of *respublica Christiana* and the transformation of the *ecclesium* into a national church and the *regnum* into what Machiavelli (1961) referred to as the *stato*, the state and states system of emergent modern Europe.

During the Reformation in many parts of north-western Europe the cosmopolitan Catholic Church was greatly reduced in its authority and power. Its *sacerdotium* was undermined and even terminated. Its lands were expropriated by kings and distributed to aristocratic supporters. Its clergy were shorn of autonomy and often reduced to being functionaries of a national church. Its parishioners were turned into a local congregation of believers cut adrift from Rome: *congregatio fidelium*. The *regnum*, however, was expanded substantially in its authority and power: it was becoming a sovereign state. Not only was it now a location of independent government but it was also a home of spiritual life as well. The king replaced the pope as head of the national church which became the church of the crown and realm. The main source of legitimate authority – religion – was now under the control of the ruler and his or her dynasty. In countries that remained Catholic the change was less dramatic and the Church had the same outward appearance as before. But over time it too became a shadow of its former self, its cosmopolitan character was diminished, and Catholic rulers, such as the kings of France and Spain, were scarcely any less independent and self-regarding in practice than their Protestant counterparts in England or Sweden. French kings, in particular, had long bridled at papal claims to supreme authority, and that was brought to an end by royal ascendancy, as indicated in chapter 3. What came to be known as the Catholic Counter-Reformation imitated the Protestant Reformation in these ways (Collinson 1993: 274–6).

The change involved taking up and putting into play new or rediscovered ideas about authority. The state monopolized all legal authority by incorporating a sovereign with a lawful right to command his or her subjects without interference from emperors or barons, popes or other prelates, either outside the country or inside. In many cases the king now claimed to rule by divine right (Figgis 1965). 'The King was regarded as the sole authority, the representative of God, to whom subjects owed a quasi-religious obedience' (Knowles 1967: 12). The king's subjects were still Christians, but church and clergy were now in the service of the crown, especially in Protestant countries. The ruler decided the religion of the realm, and thereby that of his or her subjects, according to the principle: *cujus regio ejus religio*. In England, for example, a Christian automatically became an Anglican, in Denmark and Sweden a Lutheran – not by personal choice, for they had no choice. They acquired that new identity by the dictate and at the demand of the king. In many countries the church became deeply involved with the state, not only as its source of legitimacy but also as its clerical agency: a state church: the Church of England; the Danish Lutheran Church. At a later stage in some places – for example England in the seventeenth century – 'the church' fragmented into a polyglot of particular Protestant sects and congregations. One English Protestant denomination adopted the name Congregationalist to emphasize its opposition to bishops and its advocacy of local control. Many such denominations migrated across the Atlantic and became established in colonial America, where church and state were later to become separated under the First Amendment of the United States Constitution.

But we are getting ahead of the story. There were two particularly important historical episodes in late-medieval Europe which anticipated the emergence of state sovereignty:

first, a struggle between church councils and the papacy, and second, 'concordats' (agreements, arrangements) between the papacy and secular rulers. *Respublica Christiana* presided over religious-political affairs not only by means of the papal monarchy but also by means of periodic councils of the Church, which dated back to the early Christian era when they were employed to settle doctrinal disputes. The councils and the papacy could become locked in a conflict not unlike that between parliaments and kings. Was the *sacerdotium* the papacy alone? Was it the council alone? Or was it the papacy and the council together? During the later Middle Ages various anti-papal commentators began to call for councils to place limits on what they saw as the abuse of power by certain popes who were acting more like Roman emperors – god-kings – than Vicars of Christ. Some commentators went so far as to claim that these councils possessed 'the supreme jurisdictional power of the church' on an exclusive basis (Morrall 1958: 127–8). On that reading, Church councils alone held that authority and shared it with no other ecclesiastical body, not even the papacy.[1]

The conciliar movement was provoked and emboldened in the late fourteenth and early fifteenth centuries by the simultaneous appearance of two and then three different popes each claiming to be the Vicar of Christ and presuming to embody the full and final authority of the papal monarchy. These papal rivals succeeded in producing a crisis of authority in the Church, which had to be ended if unity were to prevail. One of the most important conferences in the emergence of sovereignty was the Council of Constance, which put an end to the 'great schism' (1378–1414) by deposing the rival papal claimants and electing a new pope. This conciliar intervention in the papacy voiced some telling commentary on the question of legitimate authority in Christendom. Was the pope a constitutional monarch? Was the Church greater than the pope and was the pope merely its servant? Or was the pope ruler of the church, like an absolute monarch? Was political power a gift of God and thus subject to religious authority or was it something necessary to earthly government that could be acquired and used by secular rulers at their own discretion? The last question gets well beyond St Paul and St Augustine and anticipates Machiavelli and modern politics.

One of the most important developments of clerical diplomacy in the late Middle Ages was the settlement of outstanding ecclesiastical issues in various countries of Western Europe via bilateral agreements concluded between national monarchies and the papacy. In these 'concordats' secular rulers took upon themselves virtually an independent position vis-à-vis the pope. The concordats were almost indistinguishable from treaties, which presuppose independent organizations with authority to enter into relations on a basis of equality and reciprocity. The agreements thus give the impression of being negotiations between equal sovereign powers: international relations (Morrall 1958: 133). C. H. McIlwain (1932: 352) comments: 'the logical inference must come sooner or later that the Church is in every nation instead of embracing all nations.' If it was in every nation it was defined by the emergent states and – by implication – controlled by their rulers.

Here, then, was an early intimation of a post-medieval political world based on sovereign states as the defining and unifying institution of Europe. Their relations would be carried on bilaterally and multilaterally, via diplomacy, and would not be mediated by the papacy. Their relations would be international. Rulers would come to view each other as independent governments within their own territories. They would recognize each other. They would understand each other as having interests, which their governments were charged with defending. They would recognize that these different interests could come into conflict. They would accept that those conflicts might have to be reconciled by war if they could not be resolved via diplomacy. They would justify war as the freedom of secular sovereigns to defend their interests. War would be transformed: 'Medieval history is a history of rights and wrongs. Modern history, as contrasted with medieval, is a history of powers, forces, dynasties . . . Medieval wars are, as a rule, wars of rights; they are seldom wars of unprovoked, never wars of absolutely unjustifiable, aggression' (Hudson 1947: 3). In short, war would become monopolized by independent, self-interested, and self-justifying states.

A few late-medieval thinkers began to capture the idea of state sovereignty in their thought. As indicated, Marsiglio of Padua presented arguments, very radical at the time, for justifying the claims of secular rulers 'to exclusive control of their own affairs' (Morrall 1958: 106). Politics was held to be a worldly activity free from divine sanction. Marsiglio compared politics to an art: the state was made by leaders who mastered the art of statecraft. Gierke (1987: 92) comments: 'The steering of public affairs was likened to the steering of a ship; it is a free activity consciously directed towards the attainment of a goal. Thus there arose the idea of an Art of Government, and people undertook to teach it in detail.' Art is a free activity by definition: artists claim ownership of their work because they made it. Rulers claim full responsibility for the states they were instrumental in building, and for the laws and policies they enacted to govern them. The conception of politics as an art is hardly surprising coming from late-medieval Italians who not only produced the brilliant art of the Renaissance but also built the Italian city-states – Venice, Florence, Milan, Siena, etc. – whose beautiful public buildings were decorated with frescoes, paintings, and statues celebrating their individual identities and distinctive histories. Those political developments were already evident in the fourteenth and fifteenth centuries.

In Europe outside Italy, particularly north-western Europe, the medieval ecclesiastical-political order did not begin to fall apart until the sixteenth century under the escalating tremors of the Renaissance and the Reformation which occurred at approximately the same time. Niccolò Machiavelli was born in 1469 and Martin Luther in 1483. They came to adulthood in the early 1500s, a time that many would see as the moment of transformation. In 1532 Machiavelli wrote a famous political handbook on the new statecraft: *The Prince*. He argued, infamously at the time, that political life sometimes necessitated disobedience to the moral teachings of Christianity: personal conscience and political ethics are and must be separate (Machiavelli 1961: ch. 18). That came to be known as the political doctrine of *raison d'état*: namely that irreligious and immoral means might be necessary to achieve a desirable political goal in circumstances in which the range of choice was narrow but the value at stake was great: for instance security or survival of the state and its citizens, especially during dangerous and desperate times of war or revolution. Luther was instrumental in making the

Reformation political by justifying the independent authority of kings and the duty of Christians to obey them. That was not merely a reform of Latin Christendom. It was secession from *respublica Christiana*.

That argument in favour of freedom of rulers to set their own political course and determine the means necessary to reach their goal was, to most Christian authorities at the time, a sanction of blasphemous and criminal conduct. It must therefore be the work of the devil. Machiavelli must be the devil's servant. Christians were supposed to love their neighbours and conscientiously obey their rulers, as St Paul taught. But Machiavelli believed that in a world of flawed people one could not count on their best behaviour. Rulers were no less subject to human imperfection than other people. Yet their responsibility to give protection, to provide stability and order, was greater, indeed far greater than that of other people. That they ought to trust each other blindly or even implicitly would be a policy that could only end in disaster when that trust was betrayed, as must be expected sooner or later. The prince 'should not deviate from what is good, if that is possible, but he should know how to do evil, if that is necessary' (Machiavelli 1961: ch. 18). Machiavelli did not advocate evil for evil's sake. But he did advocate evil for politics' sake.

Other European rulers took their political cue from the Italians, and the arts and sciences of the Renaissance, including the political art of independent statecraft, spread to all of Western Europe. *Raison d'état* and more narrowly *realpolitik* or in other words the interest of the state, became a primary justification of statecraft. The 'new monarchy' was governed by a secular political craft which its officials mastered, ironically many of them clergy in the service of the king: 'Serenely conscious of their prudence, they had something of the discretion of the fonctionnaire, valuing the conduct of affairs and aware of the King's variable moods' (Mathew 1948: 10). By the sixteenth century even the papacy itself had become an independent territorial state and indeed a significant power: one among several rival powers on the Italian peninsula. If the pope was now an Italian statesman, could he still also be the presiding authority of *respublica Christiana*? Increasingly the answer given to this question was: no.

The Reformation involved a struggle for religious freedom (by Protestants) against religious orthodoxy (by Catholics) and simultaneously for political authority over religious matters – which meant freedom from foreign authority and interference, especially by the pope. The political theology of Martin Luther disengaged the authority of the state from the religious sanction of *respublica Christiana*. Luther attacked the pope's claim to hold the two swords: *sacerdotium* and *regnum*. The church's claim to be a *regnum* was excoriated as the work of the devil and a source of the corruption of the clergy. As for the *sacerdotium*, the church was nothing more than a *congregatio fidelium*: a place of worship. The true *regnum* was the state under the absolute authority of the prince; the true *sacerdotium* also belongs to the prince who is responsible for defending the Reformation in his kingdom against its enemies, internal or external. 'Luther destroyed "the metaphor of the two swords; henceforth there should be but one, wielded by a rightly advised and godly prince"' (Skinner 1978: 15). That was a revolutionary idea.

Luther recognized that his reformed Christianity and its adherents would not be safe and could not make headway without having the protection of kings and other secular rulers (Allen 1977: 19). Drawing upon St Paul's teachings on obedience to secular rulers quoted above, a text which he considered 'the most important passage in the whole Bible on the theme of political obligation' of Christian men and women, Luther preached a message of obedience and submission to secular rulers on the grounds that they were ordained by God (Skinner 1978: 14–16; Grimm 1948). Rulers maintain peace and order, and only under such conditions can the Christian word of God be preached and heard (Allen 1977: 22–3). Lutheranism became closely associated with the state and, indeed, with the notion of the divine right of kings to rule their kingdoms absolutely. In various German and Swiss cities and towns segments of the population converted to the teachings of Luther or those of other Protestant reformers, such as Calvin or Zwingli. In some places the population pre-empted the question of the state's religion and rulers acquiesced to Protestantism for the sake of political stability (Cameron 1991: 210–63). But in most principalities and kingdoms the

Reformation could not advance without the support of rulers who calculated its political advantages in addition to whatever theological attractions it might hold for them (Cameron 1991: 267–91).

That is clearly evident in Denmark and Sweden, where kings instructed their parliaments to pass laws which give them full legal control of the church in their kingdom: they terminated the legal immunities of the clergy, they abolished the independent jurisdiction of the ecclesiastical courts, they took possession of clerical lands and other church property, and they acquired the right to make all clerical appointments. The right of the papacy to confirm such appointments was rejected. In 1536 in Denmark church property along with church income (tithes) were expropriated and used to enhance the power of the monarchy which also took over the traditional social services of the church (Shennan 1974: 64). A parallel move by the king against the medieval church was made in Sweden at about the same time. The king, rather than the pope, was head of the church in the kingdom. The church was now understood to be 'a purely spiritual body, the sole duty of which was to preach the word of God without laying claim to any other powers' (Skinner 1978: 84).

In his dramatic secession from *respublica Christiana* Henry VIII of England asserted the doctrines of independence-minded kings: *rex est imperator in regno suo* (the king is emperor in his own kingdom) and *rex superiorem non recognoscens* (the king recognizes no superior). Henry obtained acts of parliament to give legal effect to these principles. The Act of Annates (1532) terminated financial transfers from English churches to the papacy. The Act of Appeals (1533) restricted severely Rome's jurisdiction over churches and clergy in England. The monasteries – which had been the most cosmopolitan of all the ecclesiastical institutions of *respublica Christiana* in England – were dissolved and the lands and rents were transferred to the crown and then distributed, in part, to the loyalist sectors of the landed aristocracy. The Act of Supremacy (1534) abolished papal authority and elevated the King to Supreme Head of the Church. The Church in England thus became the Church of England. The result has been called a 'Tudor theocracy' (Mathew 1948: 9). The Act of Supremacy reads in part:

Be it enacted by the authority of the present Parliament . . . that the King our Sovereign Lord, his heirs and successors, Kings of this realm, shall be taken, accepted and reputed the only Supreme Head in [sic] earth of the Church of England called Ecclesia Anglicana . . . Our Sovereign Lord, his heirs and successors . . . shall have full power and authority . . . to visit, repress, redress, reform, order, correct, restrain, and amend all . . . errors, heresies, abuses, offences, contempts and enormities whatsoever (Viorst 1994: 97–8).

The same assertion of sovereignty is captured by the trial of Thomas More, former Lord Chancellor of England and adviser to Henry. For refusing to take an oath which acknowledged the king's newly acquired legal authority in matters of religion, More was charged with attempting to deprive the king of his lawful title as supreme head of the Church of England, a charge of treason which carried the death penalty by beheading (Ackroyd 1999: 382–95). Church and state officials had to swear the oath of 1534 if the King's claim to supreme authority was to have both legitimacy and credibility. Thomas More could not take the oath in clear conscience because he believed that if he did so he would break faith with his Christian God and would be punished for doing so by eternal damnation. But if he kept his traditional Catholic faith he was a traitor to his king who was now the head not only of his country but also its church. 'Traitors are not condemned because they are immoral, but because they are dangerous' (Pollard 1948: 79). More made himself an enemy of his king. But had he not done so, as More understood his religious duty in accordance with medieval Latin theology, he would have been the enemy of Christ.

What previously had been a *regnum Anglicana* became a sovereign state with its own national church: the *ecclesium Anglicana* was now the Church of England. Those who had previously been Catholic clergy or parishioners were now members of Henry's church. For the vast majority of English Christians, all except leading clergy and officials, that decision was made for them by Henry. Anyone who thought otherwise opened himself or herself to the wrath of Henry. The treason laws captured the essential political idea that the king (more abstractly the state) was now above the church, and the interests of the state were prior to any demands for justice.

The temporal authorities were seen as 'Christian magistrates' who enforced the discipline of not only the state but also the church (Collinson 1993: 272). That was the doctrine of Erastianism, of state supremacy in ecclesiastical affairs, which was a hallmark of much early-modern political theory, and strikingly so in the political writings of Thomas Hobbes, probably the most outstanding theorist of the sovereign state (Hobbes 1946, 1993).

The English Reformation proved itself to be not merely a conflict between the Church of Rome and the Church of England or even between Henry and the pope. It was more fundamental: a conflict between one conception of public life organized on a cosmopolitan theological-political basis versus another constructed on the foundations of a separate kingdom, the intimation of a national state. The link with sovereignty is clear: the Reformation was instituted not via the laws of the church, canon law, but by royal decrees and parliamentary laws. Pollard (1948: 87) writes: 'The Reformation . . . is . . . the last and greatest conquest of the State, the assertion of its authority over the Church, and of its absolute, undisputed supremacy within the national frontiers.'

The political theory of sovereignty is systematically explored at length and in depth for the first time in Jean Bodin's treatise *Les six livres de la République* (1576). This was not a discourse on *respublica Christiana*. It was a theoretical treatise and book of advice on the French monarchical state as a free-standing and self-regarding political system. 'It is most expedient for the preservation of the state that the rights of sovereignty should never be granted out to a subject, still less to a foreigner, for to do so is to provide a stepping-stone where the grantee himself becomes the sovereign' (Bodin 1955: 49). That counsel was a rejection of the Middle Ages.

The discussion can be summarized. The idea of state sovereignty sorted out the uncertainty and indeed the confusion around the question of authority and law that existed in the late Middle Ages. Rulers escaped from the cosmopolitan authority of *respublica Christiana* by successfully enforcing royal authority over both church and state. The state turned territory into state property. It converted the population of that territory into subjects and later citizens. Internally, there was no room for semi-independent territory or people or institutions. Externally, there was no longer an open door to the overarching authority of pope or emperor. *Rex est imperator in regno suo.* In many places the Christian churches came under direct state control. The population of the territory now owed allegiance to the sovereign and they had a legal obligation to obey the laws of the land – even if the laws conflicted with their most deeply felt religious beliefs. In more than a few Protestant countries they often found themselves members of a state church headed by the ruler. But even in Catholic countries the church existed and carried on its activities only as long as it was underwritten by the sovereign, whose Catholicism was all-important.

It usually was only later in the modern era that monarchs and other rulers of European sovereign states extended toleration and freedom of worship to religious minorities in their countries (Jackson-Preece 1998a). Even in Britain, the most liberal country in Europe, Roman Catholics were not 'emancipated' until 1829 (Mathew 1948). That may indicate something of the prolonged fear of the sovereign rulers of Europe that the medieval theocracy was not yet finally dead.

3
Sovereigns of Europe and the World

The great transformation

The change from medieval to modern crucially involved the idea and institution of the sovereign state. Sovereignty was now vested in separate, locally controlled territorial political systems, most of them monarchies, which multiplied in both Protestant and Catholic Europe. The long-established cosmopolitan Christian Republic was disintegrating, by fits and starts, a transformation which lasted for several centuries. Driving it out of existence and taking its place was an international Europe, consisting of various rulers and their governments, each one seen to be supreme internally and independent externally. That historical transformation is clearer in hindsight than it was at the time.

When that momentous change occurred has been a subject of debate among historians. An early moment is the emergence of independent city-states and a corresponding states system on the Italian peninsula during the Renaissance in the fourteenth and fifteenth centuries.[1] Jacob Burckhardt (1992: 57–62) captured that change in a famous essay entitled 'Foreign Policy', which may be the earliest time in European history when such an expression could make any sense. He notices how these emergent city-states began to relate to each other in ways that are recognizably international, by excluding overarching religious considerations and focusing on their own interests, by negotiating as equals, and by forming expedient alliances based on those interests, even alliances with a non-Christian government, namely that of the Ottoman Turks. 'Here was no feudal system' expressing a conception of hierarchical authority. Rather, here was an international system based on the relative 'power' of each state and the adroitness of its leaders 'acting according to the exigencies of each case'.

The Italian states system was imitated by other European rulers as the Renaissance spread northwards and the Protestant Reformation began to make itself felt, at first in Germany and then across north-western Europe. At the Peace of Augsburg (1555) German Lutherans and Catholics accepted the doctrine that religious confession could not be valid grounds for military intervention: *cujus regio, ejus religio*. That placed the sovereign state above religion in matters of war. Another moment is the Dutch (Protestant) revolt and secession (1585) from Spanish (Catholic) rule in the Netherlands, which is aptly characterized as 'the successful assertion of the right of revolt against universal monarchy' (Brierly 1936: 21). That Dutch rebellion was involved with the English defeat of the Spanish naval armada shortly afterwards (1588), which was ordered by the King of Spain to restore cosmopolitan Catholic rule in Holland and England (Mattingly 1962: 69–81). There are other significant moments of transformation as well. At one extreme, Martin Wight (1977: 151) discerns its tentative beginnings in the conciliar movement of the fifteenth-century church, which restructured the papacy and circumscribed its authority, as indicated in chapter 2. At the other extreme, F. H. Hinsley (1967: 285) finds its full development only in the Concert of Europe in the 1820s, which legitimated the balance of power and the doctrine of prescription (see below) between the leading European states.

However, most scholars see the seventeenth century and particularly the peace treaties of Westphalia (1648), which settled the Thirty Years War (1618–48), as the best historical reference for symbolizing that momentous turn in European history. That episode effectively removed or led to the removal of the last vestiges of papal authority over international affairs and acknowledged the states of Europe, both Catholic and

Protestant, as independent entities. The transformation was completed and confirmed by the Peace of Utrecht (1713), which settled the War of the Spanish Succession and confirmed that the balance of power and national interests would prevail over dynastic rights in international affairs.

We should try to understand the change from the perspective of that time and not only from the present time – insofar as that is possible. The ideas and discourse available to the statesmen assembled at Münster and Osnabrück – the towns in Westphalia (north-west Germany) where the peace conference was held – were those of the late-medieval era. They understood themselves to be an assembly of Christian rulers, Protestants and Catholics, and their representatives. They had a notion of being members of one greater community the basis of which was the Christian religion. The preambles of the treaties of Münster and Osnabrück both saluted the Christian Republic: Münster in Latin (*ad Christianae Reipublicae salutem*) and Osnabrück in French (*au salut de la Republique Chrestienne*). They spoke of their peace congress as the 'senate of the Christian world'. The peace treaties do not include much specific documentary evidence for the claim that Westphalia is the crucial turning point that marks the end of the Middle Ages and the beginning of the modern world of state sovereignty.

The peacemakers were trying to reshape the political order of Europe to avoid another disastrous war. They knew they could not return to the world of 1618, even if some of them wanted to. But they knew nothing of the world that would emerge in the decades and centuries after 1648, the world they were entering and to some extent creating. We are aware of the European system and society of sovereign states that came into existence in that long and often tortuous process of change. So when we identify Westphalia as marking a momentous historical turning point, we are making an *ex post facto* analysis. We see Westphalia in the light of the modern world that subsequently emerged. From our vantage point, Westphalia is an important staging post, perhaps the most important, in a long retreat that lasted over several centuries during which time *respublica Christiana* was obliged to surrender more and more authority to the emergent states of Europe. Westphalia is best understood not as a literal moment of change but,

rather, as the symbol of a fundamental political transformation of Europe, from a transnational political-theological
world, a Catholic Christian theocracy, to a modern secular
world based on a system or society of sovereign states. That
change is, above all, a change of ideas, of thought, of how
leading Europeans conceived of their world. The old idea of
a Christian theocracy was receding into history. A revolutionary new idea of a Europe of independent states was rising in
its place.

The Peace of Westphalia was specifically concerned to end
the Thirty Years War which effectively terminated the Holy
Roman Empire as a great polity, the final incarnation of
respublica Christiana.[2] For thirty years warfare had played
havoc with large parts of the same geographical area as
present-day Germany, northern Italy, the Czech Republic,
Belgium, Luxembourg, the Netherlands, and eastern France.
Westphalia became the symbol of a post-Reformation Europe
based on mutual international recognition and intercourse of
both Protestant and Catholic states. After 1648 many political
entities of the old Empire became free-standing, self-ruling,
and self-serving to a greater extent than previously. Their
rulers became sovereigns in their own dominions: *rex est
imperator in regno suo*. They were entitled to arrange treaties
with each other and with foreign powers beyond the Empire.
The Empire still survived but as a shadow of its former self,
serving as a focus for the cultivation of ideas of German
nationalism, which eventually blossomed into political unification in the nineteenth century, when most of those older
states were unified to become modern Germany.

The pope, Innocent X, refused to accept the terms of the
Westphalian peace. He was shocked that Catholicism, and
the authority of the papacy in particular, was no longer
accorded supremacy. In his encyclical *Zelus domus Dei*
(1650), he famously vilified the agreement as 'null, void,
invalid, iniquitous, unjust, damnable, reprobate, inane, and
devoid of meaning for all time'. His intemperate denuncia-
tions could easily be dismissed. By that time the pope was a
paper tiger. That was made entirely clear in 1662 in a quarrel
between King Louis XIV of France and Pope Alexander
VII, provoked by a scuffle in Rome between the French
Ambassador and the pope's bodyguards, in which Louis broke

off diplomatic relations and threatened to invade Italy. The dispute was resolved in 1664 by the humiliating capitulation of the pope, who sent a legate to Paris to express his regret, and erected a monument in Rome which recorded the abject surrender (Pastor 1901: xxxi, 91).

By the time of the Peace of Utrecht the rulers and governments of Europe understood each other as self-determining political agents of their respective sovereign states (Osiander 1994: 120). The treaties of Westphalia and Utrecht still referred to 'Christendom' but they were among the last to do that. For what had come into historical existence in the meantime was a secular European system or society of states in which overarching political and religious authority was no longer in existence in any substantive sense. The arch constituted by *respublica Christiana* was broken and its stones lay scattered across Europe. An anarchical world of sovereign states had taken its place. Europe was composed of coexisting states that conducted their mutual political affairs via diplomacy and by reference to international law, which was understood as the law of sovereign states. When diplomacy failed, states reserved for themselves exclusively the right to wage war to resolve their conflicts. Popes could no longer authorize wars. At Utrecht these secular political and legal ideas displaced the last remnants of the political theology of Christendom.

Political philosophers and legal scholars captured the idea of a Europe of sovereign states in their treatises. In 1758 Emerich de Vattel, a Swiss diplomatist and legal theorist, framed the idea in terms that many other observers and commentators could subscribe to:

> Europe forms a political system in which the nations inhabiting this part of the world are bound together by their relations and various interests into a single body . . . The constant attention of sovereigns to all that goes on, the custom of resident ministers, the continual negotiations that take place, make modern Europe a sort of republic, whose members – each independent but all bound together by a common interest – unite for the maintenance of order and the preservation of liberty. This is what has given rise to the well-known principle of the balance of power, by which is meant an arrangement of affairs so that no state shall be in a position

to have absolute mastery and dominate over the others . . . Each independent state claims to be, and actually is, independent of all the others. (As quoted by Hinsley 1967: 166–7)

Rulers, diplomats, and commentators now spoke of 'Europe' as constituting a sphere in which the 'public good' of the states system was affirmed. The expression 'liberty of Europe' was employed to capture the same general idea. The 'public good' of Europe was defined as the 'repose' of the states and states system: the 'repose of all Europe'. 'Repose' signified a condition of peace and harmony in the relations of the sovereign states of Europe: a secular political peace which displaced the Christian cosmopolitan peace. That political transformation is what Westphalia symbolizes.

The peace and harmony of Europe was now understood as resting on 'the balance of power'. That was not analogous to a mechanical arrangement of forces that somehow occurred automatically. On the contrary, it was a political interest and goal of foreign policy. To arrange and sustain a balance of power was the highest achievement of European diplomacy and statecraft. By the eighteenth century the balance of power came to be understood as the only foundation that could ensure peace among European sovereigns. During the reign of King Louis XIV of France (in the later seventeenth century) and again at the time of Napoleon (in the late eighteenth and early nineteenth centuries) the 'liberty of Europe' was under threat from an imperious and expansionist France. In 1699 Louis expressed his understanding of the concern of rival powers about his kingdom's accumulating power and in so doing he conveyed the operative notion: 'I know how much Europe would be alarmed at seeing my own power rise above that of the House of Austria, so that this equality . . . on which it makes its repose depend would no longer obtain' (as quoted by Osiander 1994: 123).

By the eighteenth century the institution of state sovereignty had become the widely acknowledged, exclusive foundation of both domestic politics and international politics. That revolutionary political idea can be summarized:

- Europe was composed of sovereign states. Each one of those states was constitutionally prior to any treaties or international organizations they might arrange between themselves.

- European sovereigns were entitled to recognition by other European sovereigns, which involved membership in their exclusive club: the international society of Europe.
- All sovereign states were understood to have legal rights and legitimate interests.
- The legal rights were expressed in a positive law of nations – international law – that was based on the will and consent of sovereign states. International law was not a higher law above states. It was a legal arrangement of states, constructed by them in the course of their mutual relations.
- The legitimate interests were acknowledged in the practices of diplomacy: diplomats were first and foremost state representatives and agents. But diplomats were also key operatives in upholding European international society, by acting out of regard for generally accepted diplomatic practice. Diplomacy nevertheless existed primarily for the purpose of facilitating and smoothing the relations of sovereign states.
- While sovereign states controlled their own means of power – military and economic – which varied enormously from one country to the next, they were expected to exercise that power responsibly, which meant that they were supposed to operate in accordance with international law and diplomatic practice.
- Those vitally important states, the great powers, were expected to employ their compelling military might, economic clout, and political prestige to uphold and not to disrupt the balance of power. They were the guarantors of the peace and harmony of Europe. If any great power acted in a manner that threatened or upset the balance of power, it could expect to be confronted by a military coalition of other great powers determined to cut it down to size.

Although simplified for purposes of exposition, these were foundation elements of the idea of state sovereignty as it emerged out of the debris of the medieval Christian empire. They have not changed significantly in the past three centuries.

However, during that period the locus, uses, justifications, and varieties of sovereignty have changed, with new ones adopted and old ones abandoned.

As indicated in chapter 1, sovereignty is a relatively simple idea that states can use to build almost anything with, large or small, as long as they follow the rules. Sovereignty has resided in kings and royal families (dynastic sovereignty), imperial powers and their colonial agents (imperial sovereignty), national parliaments and assemblies (parliamentary sovereignty), and the whole citizen body of a country (popular sovereignty). The same state can be sovereign in different ways in different places. In the early twentieth century the British House of Commons was at one and the same time the central institution of both parliamentary sovereignty in the United Kingdom and imperial sovereignty in numerous British colonies around the world. Sovereignty has been employed to establish empires and hold colonies. It has been used to condemn imperialism, to demand decolonization, and to establish new states in place of colonies. The justifications of sovereignty have been religious and secular, monarchical and republican, aristocratic as well as democratic. Smaller sovereign states have been submerged or united in greater sovereign states (Italy, Germany). Larger sovereign states (Western empires) have been partitioned into smaller ones, or a regional segment (the American colonies) of a larger state (the British Empire) has seceded and established itself on an independent basis. Sovereignty discloses other arrangements besides these.

The divine right of kings

Governments require legitimacy and legality to be stable and effective over the longer term. Power alone is not sufficient. Faced with that problem in a world that continued to be under the sway of religious ideas, the new sovereigns of Europe came up with the doctrine of the divine right of kings. It asserts that monarchical governments are legitimate and lawful in God's eyes without any seal of papal or clerical confirmation. It proclaims a divorce of *rex* (king) and *regna* (kingdom) from *respublica Christiana*. But it is a bonding between a ruler and God: it is godly rule via the king. In this way of thinking kings are directly God's agents on earth; to perform that role they do not have to call upon the church. They are sovereign on earth because God made them so. Henry VIII is sovereign because he is carrying out God's plan and executing God's will. Henry must therefore be obeyed absolutely – regardless of what the pope or other religious leaders command – for otherwise one is disobeying God. The doctrine is thus one of 'obedience from motives based on religion' (Figgis 1965: 51).

The doctrine proved to be compelling and useful for independence-minded post-medieval rulers because it was, at the same time, intelligible and meaningful to their principal subjects and very expedient for the justification of kingship. It was a convenient and timely marriage between religious belief and political utility. Here theology was at the service of politics in a particularly effective way. The doctrine was seized upon as a formulation of sovereignty that people of the day could understand and take on board the new ship of state. It proved effective because the vast majority still thought of themselves as God's creatures, still understood political life as well as family life and all other aspects of their personal and social existence in Christian terms. They were inclined to obey political authority if it could credibly and convincingly claim God's sanction. That is what the doctrine set out to do and largely achieved. King James I of England (1603–25) put the point in memorable terms in a speech to parliament in 1609: 'Kings are not only God's lieutenants upon earth and sit upon God's throne, but even by God himself they are called gods . . . they have power of raising and casting down, of life and of death, judges over all their subjects and in all causes and yet accountable to none but God only' (James I: 1609).

Post-medieval kings were imitating medieval popes. Papal claims to divine rulership over Christendom contained all the essential elements of the doctrine of divine right: the idea of a sovereign state in the shape of the papal monarchy; the idea that unity in a state is only to be secured by absolute supremacy of one authority; the argument that sovereignty is vested in a single person by God and must therefore be obeyed; and the assertion that disobedience of the sovereign and resistance to his commands is a mortal sin. The crucial difference was that there were now many divine kingships in Europe and no longer only one, and all of them were God's lieutenants, presumably even when they waged war against each other.

With the advent of the Protestant Reformation this theory and practice of state sovereignty became conceivable and opportune for kings. If they wished to rule independently with a claim to legitimacy and legality that could be understood and accepted, it was not enough for rulers merely to assert some secular basis for their authority: for example, the rights of custom and convention, the rights of inheritance, the rights of dynastic marriage. All those rights were significant but they were not sufficient to underwrite the new monarchies in what was still a religious era. Kings could now assert that they ruled by recognized right of the highest authority of all: the Christian God. There could not be two divine rulers in one body politic, any more than there could be more than one Christian God. There could only be one such ruler and kings, such as Henry VIII, were determined to be that singular godly ruler in their own realm. Kings had to be obeyed because they were carrying out God's plan for humankind. Popes had to be disobeyed, for they were interlopers who were interfering with God's law.

Later it was necessary to find other grounds for sovereign authority of secular governments to take the place of the legitimate and legal right of kings and dynasties, when the latter's claims and assertions of authority could no longer be accepted. Here 'the people' began to come into view as the basis of state sovereignty. What proved to be morally decisive in defying the king, or at least curbing royal authority and power, was the claim that sovereignty was a trust from the people. An early example was the Dutch revolt against Spanish rule in the sixteenth century. The States-General of the Netherlands declared that 'a prince is constituted by God to be ruler of a people, to defend them from oppression and violence'. If instead the prince abuses them, 'then he is no longer a prince but a tyrant, and they may not only disallow his authority, but legally proceed to the choice of another prince for their defence' (as quoted by Wight 1977: 155).

That same assertion of popular sovereignty was also evident during the English Civil War (1642–9). In late 1648 King

Charles I was captured by the parliamentary and anti-royalist army of Oliver Cromwell, held prisoner, and brought to justice. His trial in January 1649 was an occasion for the making of particularly explicit arguments concerning legitimate and lawful state authority. On one side stood Charles, the son of King James I, who defended himself in terms of the divine right of kings. On the other side stood his parliamentary enemies, who prosecuted him in terms of popular consent.

The king's argument, briefly stated, ran as follows. Cromwell and his political and military supporters claimed that the will of the government and its authority rested in the people on whose behalf they were acting. But for Charles that was an arrogant and contemptuous assertion that defied God and all Christian teaching on the lawful authority of kings. The assertion was outrageous and indeed blasphemous, for it scorned God's instructions on the responsibilities of the subjects of kings, which was absolute obedience to lawful kingship. Charles reminded his captors and accusers that there was no English law in existence that authorized the trial of a lawful king by his subjects. And Charles was the lawful king of England. The king alone possessed sovereign authority which was sacred and which God had entrusted him with. True sovereignty was vested in the king by God. 'Remember I am your King . . . your lawful king . . . I have a trust committed to me by God' (as quoted by Wedgwood 1964: 131).

Charles's argument that all law and justice proceeded from the godly sovereign was difficult to contend with in a political and social universe still animated by Protestant Christianity. The prosecution endeavoured to overcome that obstacle by asserting the sovereignty of the people and claiming that parliament and the parliamentary army that captured Charles and brought him to trial were its representatives and agents. There was a more fundamental law that Charles was duty bound to defend and uphold, and 'the Parent or Author of the Law . . . is the People of England' (Wedgwood 1964: 122, 129). Charles had subverted 'the ancient and fundamental laws and liberties of this nation'. He had contrived a plot 'to enslave the English nation' and had waged war on his subjects, which was an act of 'treason'. He had conspired 'to erect and uphold in himself an unlimited and tyrannical power to rule according to his Will, and to overthrow the Rights and Liberties of the People' (Prosecution charge quoted by Wedgwood 1964: 130).

> There is a contract and a bargain made between the King and his people, and your oath is taken: and certainly, Sir, the bond is reciprocal: for as you are the liege lord, so they liege subjects. . . . This we know now, the one tie, the one bond, is the bond of protection that is due from the sovereign; the other is the bond of subjection that is due from the subject. Sir, if this bond be once broken, farewell sovereignty! (Prosecution statement as quoted by Wedgwood 1964: 161)

King Charles I was found guilty and was publicly beheaded for his high crimes.

Here, then, is an early and bloody instance of the doctrine of popular sovereignty, of the social contract between ruler and ruled. It was not made in the tranquillity of a philosopher's study: Hobbes, Locke, and Rousseau had yet to publish their celebrated treatises on the subject.[3] Rather, it was registered in the tumult of compelling political circumstance, during a bitter civil war, to deal with an urgent problem of legitimating state authority to vindicate Oliver Cromwell's military victories over the royalist armies of Charles, to justify the abolition of the monarchy, and to sanction Cromwell's installation as sovereign ruler of the English people. Viewed in retrospect, it was a sign of things to come.

Sir Robert Filmer is famous for attempting, very late in the day, to provide some historical and philosophical rationalization to bolster the Stuart dynasty's divine and absolute right to rule England. In his book *Patriarcha* he asserts that English monarchs have such a right because they are in a direct line of descent reaching back to Adam and the Jewish kings of the Old Testament of the Bible. The argument was routed by John Locke in his famous treatise on civil government, which portrayed sovereignty as resting exclusively on a social contract in which the government was beholden to the governed who could legitimately and lawfully rebel against a tyrant (Locke 1965). But that new doctrine did not displace the older doctrine across Europe until much later. The divide between the divine right of kings and the sovereignty of the people was bridged, historically, by dynastic sovereignty based on prescription, which prevailed in most of Europe until the nineteenth century, and even down to the end of the First World War in some places.

Dynastic sovereignty

The doctrine of the divine right of kings was useful only in a certain kind of society in which the majority believed implicitly in God's power and right to command them, and their duty to obey 'Him'. If that belief began to erode seriously, it would lose whatever political efficacy it once might have possessed. That happened in the seventeenth and eighteenth centuries when some Europeans and the Dutch, English, and French in particular began to see religion as a matter less of state authority and more of private conscience, and to assert and accept other grounds for vindicating state sovereignty.

In the first chapter it was noted that the term 'sovereignty' signified, among other things, 'a territory under the rule of a sovereign, or existing as an independent state'. In that conception there is an important distinction between a ruler and a state. 'In the original theory', as Brierly (1936: 36) points out, 'it was not the state that was sovereign, but a person or persons within a state that were "sovereign" over the rest.' The sovereign was the ruler, typically a monarch and his or her dynasty. That was in accordance with the derivation of the word from the Latin *superanus*, meaning 'superior'. The notion of superiority later became that of supreme authority within the state, which is one of the two defining features of 'sovereignty', as noted. States, as such, were once understood as alternatives to monarchies as a form of government, as indicated by the existence in Holland of an 'Estates-General' form, in Switzerland of a confederal form, and in Venice of a republican form of government. Those polities were 'sovereign' states without being monarchies. That eventually became the standard concept.

For a lengthy period, however, dynastic sovereignty prevailed in European politics. Once kings and their families and descendants could establish their claim to supreme authority as valid in itself, without any reference to God or anyone else, sovereignty began to disclose itself as a purely secular form of authority residing in a dynasty's exclusive, prescriptive rights to rule. Here 'secular' means free from religious validation or theological concerns. In the era of dynastic sovereignty the ruler and the royal family became 'a caste apart' (Pollard 1948: 70) which was raised above all other families in the kingdom by its title to rule. It was only equalled by other ruling dynasties of the European states system. When monarchs claimed to rule legitimately and lawfully by heredity, by inheritance, by marriage contract, etc. without need of any other grounds for their authority, either religious or popular, it is an indication that has happened.

Such claims are conventionally labelled as 'prescriptive' (Wight 1977: 157). 'Prescription' should be understood as a claim or title or right to something based on long use or enjoyment of it. It also contains the further idea of *ex injuria jus oritur*: 'an act of violence and injustice, by lapse of time and some degree of acceptance, could give rise to rights' (Wight 1977: 163). Territory seized by war and conquest, and successfully held over a period of time, could be held by right. Prescription was thus another word for possession, proprietary right, and, indeed, ownership: a lawful title of possession of a territory, a right to control its affairs and, to that end, to command its population who were the subjects of the sovereign ruler: the king's or the queen's subjects.

In the early-modern era sovereignty became attached to a ruler and his or her dynasty via the institution of hereditary monarchy. Elizabeth I was the sovereign of England (1558–1603) in virtue of being the successor to that office controlled at the time by the Tudor dynasty of which she allegedly was the leading member. When she died, unmarried and without any legitimate heirs, the title of English sovereign passed to the Stuart dynasty of Scotland. But even in the sixteenth and seventeenth centuries sovereignty was never completely personal or exclusively dynastic. The King or Queen of England was sovereign over a kingdom or realm: that is, a state. If there was no realm there could be no sovereign in the complete political sense of the word. The ruler had a mortal lifespan, and the dynasty survived for as long as it could – several generations or a few centuries. But the realm was, so to speak, perpetual. One of the earliest intimations of sovereignty and one of the most important ideas of political thought is the distinction between *rex* and *regnum*: the king had two bodies: his personal body and the body politic (Kantorowicz 1957). The king is mortal and will die but the state is enduring. Sovereignty fundamentally concerns the body politic and not the body of the king or queen.

The proprietary right vested in dynastic sovereignty is captured concisely by Ludwig von Mises (1983: 31): 'The political conception of the princely state is the interest of the ruler.' We could equally say defending the interest of the state is the responsibility of the ruler. This disarmingly simple formulation sums up an idea of autocracy and absolutism which dominated European politics until the nineteenth century and lingered on until the early twentieth century in some places. The population was resources and instruments of the state, the basis of state power, 'a mass of subjects whose nationality had no political significance' (Ritter 1976: 47). When territories were acquired, by conquest or dynastic marriage, their populations were acquired at the same time; consequently in the European dynastic state rulers and ruled often came from entirely different ethno-linguistic groups. Rulers and their representatives and agents typically spoke French but their subjects spoke local vernacular languages: Russian, Polish, Flemish, Hungarian, Slovakian, Slovenian, etc.

The age of dynastic sovereignty was usually marked by the demotion and sometimes even the dissolution of previously semi-autonomous communities and corporations which were the legacy of European feudalism, such as landed nobility, self-governing towns, self-regulating universities, self-directing guilds, and so forth. It was the triumph of ruling dynasties to rise above feudal particularisms and if necessary even to suppress them in order to establish royal authority, the crown, throughout their jurisdictions, over all their subjects, and free from previously intervening authorities. Dynastic sovereigns were also characterized by their use of crown privileges, grants, licences, and other dispensations issued to individuals or groups to enhance their authority and control over important social and economic sectors of the population (Spengler 1964: 45–6). One of the best examples of European absolutism was France in the seventeenth century. Jean Colbert (1619–83), chief adviser to King Louis XIV (1643–1715), was the leading architect of a unified and powerful French monarchy (by the standards of that era) in which autonomous communities and corporations, including the church, were subordinated successfully and permanently to the crown (Clark 1960: 69–70).

Gerhard Ritter (1976: 6) comments: the state was 'essentially a dynastic construction; only rarely and from a distance could the subjects' wishes, longings, and fears make themselves heard in the realm of policy.' Here is the hallmark of dynasticism, which dominated European statecraft for almost three centuries, and was 'still alive at the three European imperial courts [Vienna, Berlin and St Petersburg] until the . . . upheavals [of the First World War]' (von Mises 1983: 31). In these cases dynastic sovereignty and imperial sovereignty were difficult if not impossible to disentangle. Dynastic statecraft aimed at enabling the empire at least to survive if not to expand, permitting the current trustees of the royal patrimony to pass it on to their successors, if not enlarged then at least not diminished from what it had been when they inherited it.

Dynasticism was an international system based on the royal families of Europe, whose solidarity was established and reinforced not only by doctrine and precedent but also by intermarriage. The dynasties, taken together, formed the ruling caste of Europe whose leading members operated with 'a dynastic idiom of international politics' in which 'alliances were consolidated by dynastic marriages' and 'reversals of alliance were marked by matrimonial disengagements' (Wight 1977: 154). The most emblematic and probably also the most successful European dynasty was the Habsburgs. Their extensive territories (which in the sixteenth century already reached across the Atlantic into Central and South America) were ultimately the property not of the peoples who lived in them but of the state held in trust by the ruling family. It is perhaps not surprising, then, that their motto was *Austriae est imperatura orbi universo* (Austria is universal world empire).

Dynastic sovereignty, resting on prescription, acquired perhaps its final definition at the Congress of Vienna (1814–15) which contemplated the succession question in

France that was created by the military defeat of Napoleon. Talleyrand, the French representative, expressed the idea in one of his memoirs: 'A lawful government . . . is always one whose existence, form and mode of action, has been consolidated and consecrated by a long succession of years . . . The legitimacy of the sovereign power results from the ancient status of possession, just as, for private individuals, does the right of property' (as quoted by Osiander 1994: 214). For Talleyrand, the point of upholding prescription as the definitive claim to sovereignty was to ensure political stability, both domestic stability in France and international stability in Europe, and to avoid revolutionary struggles over the control of the state, which very likely would provoke foreign intervention and war. Prescription was conducive to peace and was in everybody's interests. The institution of dynastic sovereignty among the great powers was considered to be the best insurance for European order, both domestically and internationally.

The interest of the ruler, dynasty, and empire (which amounted to the same thing) was the overriding object of statecraft, which involved a body of precepts intended for the advantage and service of the state. Everything and everybody, including the clergy, was subordinate to it. John Seldon, a leading English legal commentator of the mid-seventeenth century, made the point succinctly: 'all is as the State pleases.' He did not say that about the monarch or the royal family, only about the state. As indicated in chapter 2, this sovereignty doctrine (Erastianism) held that the state is supreme over the church (Wood 1967), and even that religion is 'the creature of the state' (Figgis 1965: 57).

The dynastic doctrine began to merge into a doctrine of solely state sovereignty in the eighteenth century, as indicated by the political commentaries of King Frederick II ('the Great') of Prussia (1740–86) written towards the end of his reign. A king's claim to authority derived from the state and reflected the right and dignity of the state – which was not the same as the dynasty. In Frederick's state, dynastic and personal consideration had no place, just as the sectional interests of his various subjects had no place. The people at large also had no place. The state had its own life and its own purposes, which stood far above the opinions of individuals or groups or even entire populations that were subject to it. Frederick portrayed himself as 'the servant' of the state and his policy as guided by *raison d'état*. Frederick was a hereditary monarch. But he disavowed the notion that he was above everybody and that he, personally, was the state: a famous assertion made by French King Louis XIV. Rather, Frederick saw himself as the leading representative and agent of the state. The ruler's first and foremost duty was to the state: the king was the 'first servant' of the state. Both prince and people were its servants. Both domestic policy and foreign policy were to be guided exclusively by *raison d'état*, by the rational interests of the impersonal state. That idea of an impersonal, sovereign state to which everybody was subordinate, including the king, eventually carried the day.

Western empires

After Westphalia Western Europe came to understand itself as a world of sovereign states which, although they were unequal in terms of population, territory, military power, and economic wealth, were all equal in terms of international law and diplomacy. They were all part of the same international society, which was their exclusive club. They regularly waged war and conquered segments of each other's territory, but they did not extinguish each other's sovereignty. Very few of these states suffered the fate of Poland, which was partitioned by the great powers on several occasions, the final one by Austria, Prussia, and Russia in 1795. That was met with shock and anger from those who considered it a violation of European civilization. The remarks of Edmund Burke and those of Lord Acton are indicative (Himmelfarb 1962: 136):

> No wise or honest man can approve of that partition or can contemplate it without prognosticating great mischief from it to all countries at some future time . . .

> The partition of Poland was an act of wanton violence, committed in open defiance not only of popular feeling but of public law. For the first time in modern history a great State

was suppressed, and a whole nation divided among its enemies . . .

Thus, in the relations of sovereign states to each other, Westphalia overthrew the practices of imperialism. Constitutional developments in Europe set a course that eventually led to parliamentary sovereignty and on to popular sovereignty.

The story beyond Europe followed a different and older course. In the relations of European states to political authorities in the rest of the world Westphalia initially reiterated and reinforced a doctrine of the superiority of Christian cum European civilization, the moral inequality of peoples, the right of intervention, the right of conquest, and ultimately the right of colonization. The old medieval boundary between Christendom and the non-Christian world, which itself succeeded that between the Roman Empire and the barbarian world, was redefined yet again, now as a line between the civilized European cum Western world and the not yet fully or properly civilized rest of the world. Only much later, in the mid-twentieth century, did Westphalia become a universal idea of a global society of sovereign states that equally embraced or at least tolerated all religions, civilizations, cultures, and races without significant exception.

Before that time indigenous authorities in the Americas, Asia, Africa, the Middle East, and the Pacific were rarely recognized or respected by European states – ever more so, as the military and commercial power of those states became more and more compelling. European governments saw commercial and military advantages in acquiring and holding non-European territory. They were in a position to do that owing to the scientific, technological, and industrial revolutions that their progress-minded and innovative peoples had set in train. To count as a significant European state it became necessary to have an empire. Many states, eventually even small states such as Belgium, successfully projected military power and business enterprises into non-European areas, where they inevitably made contact and frequently came into conflict with indigenous authorities, which they usually came to dominate.

European imperialism was typically justified on the grounds that non-European authorities were unqualified to possess and unfit to exercise state sovereignty (Bain 2003). That was a Eurocentric judgement, of course, but it was more complicated than that implies because there was a genuine problem of determining which way to respond to non-European authorities once European states became involved with them on a more regular basis. The problem briefly stated was: how could alien non-Western authorities and populations be integrated into the Eurocentric but now globalizing system of sovereign states? They could not be integrated as equal member states owing to their deep differences in civilization, religion, culture, race, language, etc., all of which was seen as profoundly alien to European civilization. For largely the same reason those authorities could not be bypassed and their populations integrated directly into the metropolitan sovereignty of intervening European states by extending citizenship to them. That would have been inconceivable in any case – although France did extend metropolitan citizenship to a few Africans and Asians in its colonies. Yet those indigenous authorities and populations could not be left alone, either, because the expanding European states system had come into contact with them, had to deal with them, and had interests in them and concerns about them. It was therefore necessary, if not obligatory, to fit them into the system somehow. The fallback and traditional solution was by taking control of them as imperial or quasi-imperial dependencies of one kind or another (Wight 1952: 5–14). International law as well as *realpolitik* made ample provision for that option.

Empire-building by European states was the fashion from the seventeenth century until the early twentieth century. Indeed, the high water mark was the late nineteenth century when the territorial extent of European imperialism was at its greatest. It is not my purpose to investigate European empires in any detail but merely to identify imperialism as among the evolving ideas and institutions of state sovereignty. However, it may be useful to take note of the most important European empires that were built and sustained during that era.

The first to notice are those of Spain and Portugal which were already being contemplated in the late fifteenth century. They followed and even accompanied the *reconquista* (reconquest) of Granada (southern Spain) from the Islamic Moors – in what arguably was the last medieval Christian crusade – and the discovery of the 'new world' by the Italian navigator Christopher Columbus, both historical events occurring in the same remarkable year, 1492. European conquest and colonization beyond Europe was initially sanctioned by the *respublica Christiana*. Just one year after Columbus's sensational achievement, King Ferdinand and Queen Isabella of Spain asked Pope Alexander VI to intercede as the Supreme Judge of Christendom in a dispute between the Spanish and Portuguese crowns concerning sovereignty over the new world. He issued the Bull (edict) *Inter Caetera* (1493) which solemnly proclaimed a righteous and lawful partition of the world between the rival powers (*Catholic Encyclopedia Online*). Spain was allocated all lands to the west and Portugal all lands to the east of a meridian in the Atlantic Ocean that was drawn a hundred leagues (approximately 300 miles or 500 kilometres) west of the Cape Verde Islands and the Azores.

At that time European rulers could still seek the authority of the pope on questions of title to territory. But the notion that territorial occupations could be authorized by anyone other than European sovereigns themselves – that medieval notion disappeared, for all practical purposes, in the sixteenth century. It was not long before the Dutch, with the English and the French hot on their heels, were taking possession of overseas territories in accordance with the then novel and still unsettled law of nations. Later the Russians and others also became involved in the competition for non-Western empires.

A brief glance at the political map of the world in the early eighteenth century (Darby and Fullard 1979: 8–9) indicates that the territorial sovereignty of various imperialist European states had been established in many places outside Europe. The Portuguese empire stretched along the Atlantic coast of South America and along both the western and the eastern coasts of Southern Africa. The Spanish empire extended uninterrupted from Mexico in the north to Chile in the south of what had come to be known as Spanish America, with additional territories in the Caribbean and the Philippines. The Dutch empire was already operating in South Asia and South-East Asia with other territories in the Americas and at the tip of southern Africa on the Cape of Good Hope. The British

Empire was well established on the east coast of North America, in the Caribbean, on coastal locations in West Africa, South Asia, and South-East Asia. The French empire extended from the Atlantic coast of North America up the St Lawrence river, into the Great Lakes, and down the Mississippi river to the gulf coast and into the Caribbean, with coastal enclaves in West Africa and island territories in the Indian Ocean. The Russian empire was pushing into the Middle East in the Caucasus, had stretched across Siberia to the Pacific Ocean, and would soon cross the Bering Sea into North America and eventually reach what today is northern California.

The British empire was the most extensive geographically of all modern empires, indeed of all empires ancient, medieval, and modern. The English push into the non-European world got underway in earnest in the mid-sixteenth century (Lloyd 1984: 1–29). By the second half of the seventeenth century they were well established in North America and would be contending with the French for continental supremacy. In the Seven Years War (1756–63) Britain wrested strategic control of the continent by defeating France. No sooner had they celebrated their great triumph when they were confronted by an armed rebellion in their Atlantic seaboard colonies, suffering an astonishing military defeat at the hands of their upstart American cousins in the War of Independence (1776–83) which resulted in the surrender of British imperial sovereignty over all thirteen colonies. However, they still exercised sovereignty over a reduced British North America (Canada and Newfoundland) and many islands in the Caribbean. By that time Britain was moving towards supremacy in India and other parts of South and South-East Asia. In the nineteenth century Britain was the world's leading industrial power; had the largest navy, which commanded the sea lanes of the world; dominated world trade with London, the centre of international finance, and was moving towards a predominant imperial position in Africa and the Middle East.

The British Empire at its highest point is an excellent example of a conglomerate state consisting of its homeland, Great Britain and Ireland, the British Dominions (Canada, Australia, New Zealand, South Africa), British India, and an assortment of crown colonies (settled colonies, conquered colonies, and ceded colonies), colonial protectorates, protected states, and mandated (trust) territories located in different continents and oceans around the world (Wight 1952: 5–14). British imperial sovereignty was arranged in various ways, depending on circumstances but depending most of all on how the dependency was acquired in the first place. Although the diversity of dependencies of the British Empire is noteworthy, the fundamental point about imperial sovereignty remained: in spite of the different degrees of local control in the various dependencies Britain remained firmly in overall control. And before any of those dependencies could become sovereign, the British government would have to relinquish and transfer sovereignty to them. The British Empire lasted until the mid-twentieth century, after which time it was rapidly dismantled, along with all other Western empires, in the face of accelerating, worldwide demands for decolonization based on the claim of popular sovereignty. But as late as 1939 its diverse territories and peoples were scattered across the entire world: schoolchildren not only in Britain but also in Canada, Australia, New Zealand, South Africa, India, Malaya, Jamaica, and many other such places were taught that 'the sun never sets on the British empire'. Very shortly afterwards the imperial sun did indeed set, forever.

The law of nations became clarified, in part, out of those European imperial endeavours, in response to important issues such as rights of territorial acquisition and freedom of the seas. Spanish jurisprudence contributed to emergent international law via important commentaries by Antonia Montesinos, Francisco de Vitoria, and Bartolomé de Las Casas, among other Dominicans, who addressed the issue of the right of the Spanish *conquistadores* to take possession of lands in the Americas occupied by the Aztecs and the Incas and to subject those conquered peoples to Spanish sovereignty (Pennington 1970; Parry 1966: 57–60). The now famous question raised by those Dominicans was: 'Are These not also Men?' (Seed 1993). Here is the earliest stirring of the doctrine of self-determination which eventually came to justify state sovereignty everywhere across the world. Hugo Grotius (2005) argued that the high seas, so necessary to Dutch commerce and prosperity, could not become part of the territorial jurisdiction of any state. John Seldon replied by defending English territorial claims over certain seas (Brierly 1936: 190).

Imperial sovereignty

The central focus of imperial sovereignty is what international legal scholars term 'territorial sovereignty'. That idea (discussed at greater length in chapter 4) arises from the reality that states are earth-bound organizations in the most fundamental sense. They could not exist without bordered territory which is, so to speak, the foundation upon which they rest and the spatial sphere within which they exercise authority: 'jurisdiction over persons and things to the exclusion of the jurisdiction of other states' (Brierly 1936: 119). Title to territory in international law resembles the right of ownership in private law. Classical international lawyers did indeed borrow rules governing the domestic acquisition of property from Roman law (Nicholas 1987: 98–157). In acquiring non-European territory the European states were indeed guided by Roman principles and practices: by occupation of *terra nullius* (territory not already under the jurisdiction of any sovereign state or other subject of international law), by cession (the yielding up of a territory), by prescription (holding and using a territory over time), by inheritance, and by war and conquest. That is clearly evident in the British Foreign Jurisdiction Acts (1890, 1913) which laid down, in arch legalese, rules for the acquisition and control of foreign territory:

> Whereas by treaty, capitulation, grant usage, sufferance and other lawful means, Her Majesty the Queen has jurisdiction within divers foreign countries . . . It is and shall be lawful for Her Majesty the Queen to hold, exercise, and enjoy any jurisdiction which Her Majesty now has or may at time hereafter have within a foreign country in the same and as ample manner as if Her Majesty had acquired that jurisdiction by the cession or conquest of territory. (as quoted by Wight 1952: 550)

What is the point of going into the international law of territorial sovereignty and the domestic law of foreign jurisdiction? Because that is where the historically important notion of imperial sovereignty is most clearly and completely set out. When European states began to penetrate non-European continents and oceans in the early-modern era, usually in competition with each other, the question of title to territory arose: both in relation to each other and in relation to the non-European political systems that occupied those territories. Sovereignty was conveniently available as an institution for taking legal possession of foreign territory in an orderly fashion.

European imperialists understandably preferred a legal title to territory, rather than the uncertainty of holding it by force in competition with each other. They consequently were inclined to recognize each other's empires, according to the principle of reciprocity, while not recognizing most non-European political authorities. They arrived at the latter position after a period of uncertainty when their power was insufficient to impose their political will on resisting indigenous governments outside Europe. Before that happened, during the early period of European imperialism, there was a willingness to recognize the sovereignty of non-Western rulers in accordance with the doctrine of natural law. Alexandrowicz (1969: 469) draws attention to the fact that

> Grotius, in his work on Freedom of the Sea (1608) speaks . . . of East Indian Sovereigns who allied themselves with some of the European powers. It is through the study of these alliances and treaties of a commercial and political character, and of the diplomatic missions dealing with their conclusion and implementation, that the position of East Indian Sovereigns in the pre-nineteenth century Family of Nations can be properly assessed. Grotius has no hesitation in calling their sovereign status in the Law of Nations by its proper name.

Natural law, rooted in ancient and medieval jurisprudence, was later displaced by positive law – such as the British Foreign Jurisdiction Acts – as the basis for European claims to territorial sovereignty in non-Western areas of the world. Positive law was the law European sovereign states created for themselves. That restriction of rights of territorial sovereignty almost entirely to European and later Western states occurred once they became sufficiently powerful to brush indigenous non-European authorities aside. In that way, via European imperialism, sovereignty became a global institution. Even where non-European authorities could not be completely subjected to imperial sovereignty, as in the case of China, Western states nonetheless employed their military and commercial power and the international law of the day to handicap indigenous authorities. Even the anti-imperialist United States, in an 1844 'Treaty of Peace, Amity and Commerce' with China, demanded and received extraterritorial jurisdiction which excluded American citizens in China from Chinese authority. Other Western states made similar treaty arrangements for their nationals in China. That has been aptly termed 'non-territorial imperialism' (Ruskola 2005) which in the foregoing example lasted for a full century.

Non-European authorities were almost always regarded as lacking valid claims to sovereignty and were accordingly subjected to unequal treaties and other discriminatory measures by European intruders. The justification for that discrimination had a medieval echo: it was the right and indeed the responsibility of Europeans to rule non-Europeans and other peoples of different and by implication lesser religion or civilization than their own. There was believed to be a 'standard of civilization', to which non-Western societies had to measure up, before they could make a credible claim to state sovereignty (Gong 1984: part I). The high point of European imperial sovereignty, in this regard, was reached in the second half of the nineteenth century. It is captured in the attitude of a prominent British international lawyer in 1880:

> It is scarcely necessary to point out that as international law is a product of the special civilization of modern Europe, and forms a highly artificial system of which the principles cannot be supposed to be understood or recognized by countries differently civilized, such states can only be presumed to be subject to it. (W.E. Hall, as quoted by Wight 1977: 115)

In the second half of the nineteenth century, under the influence of Social Darwinism and other European and American doctrines of racial superiority, the authority, rights, and privileges associated with state sovereignty became defined in terms of advanced and backward peoples. Sovereignty could only be conferred on people who could handle it, and those people predictably turned out to be members of the white race. 'The expansion of England could be explained only in terms of the heroic qualities of the English race and their natural genius for government' (Hannaford 1996: 286). Woodrow Wilson – when he was still a professor of political science at Princeton University and well before he became President of the United States – expressed the view that good governance reflected the racial characteristics of people, and 'it is Aryan [i.e. the white race] practice we principally wish to know' (as quoted by Hannaford 1996: 345). Because sovereignty entailed the most basic rights and the heaviest responsibilities, it was necessary to ensure that it was conferred on rulers and peoples who were fit for it. Fitness was ultimately defined in racial terms.

That idea of racially exclusive sovereignty understandably provoked a profound and fully justified reaction in the assertion of racial equality, which eventually triumphed (Mazrui 1967). Before that finally happened the idea of being racially unfit was displaced by the notion of being not yet sufficiently prepared educationally and equipped economically and technologically for the heavy burdens of independent self-government. That was expressed by colonial policies and embodied in international agreements marked by ideas of trusteeship (Bain 2003). That was the notion that Europeans and Americans must govern Asians, Africans, Pacific and Indian Ocean peoples, and other non-Western indigenous peoples with their best interests in view, until such time as those peoples were able to govern themselves.

Europeans and Americans were the only ones who could decide when their non-Western subjects reached political maturity. That is evident in the General Act of the Berlin Conference (1884–5) which sanctioned the partition of Africa and called upon 'all the Powers exercising sovereign rights [in the continent] . . . to watch over the preservation of the native tribes, and to care for the improvement of the conditions of their moral and material well-being . . . bringing home to them the blessings of civilization' (Art. VI). It is evident in the League of Nations Mandates System which spoke of 'peoples not yet able to stand by themselves under the strenuous conditions of the modern world' whose 'tutelage' 'should be entrusted to advanced nations' (Art. 22). And it is evident in the United Nations Trusteeship Council which aimed 'to promote the political, economic, social, and educational advancement of the inhabitants of trust territories, and their progressive development towards self-government or independence as may be appropriate in the particular circumstances of each territory and its peoples' (Art. 76).

What proved fatal to the institution of imperial sovereignty was the liberal idea that there was something inherently wrong about a government that laid claim to foreign territories and populations without their uncoerced consent – even if its intentions were benevolent. The society of sovereign states was now understood as an association in which membership could not be denied on grounds of religion, civilization, culture, race, or development. That presupposed an intrinsic and prior right to sovereignty that is usually portrayed as a right of national self-determination and self-government. In spite of the thorny practical problem of determining who ought to exercise that right or in other words what is the 'nation' for purposes of political independence in particular cases – which is anything but easy to figure out – that came to be virtually the only valid ground for claiming state sovereignty in what had been Western overseas imperial territories.

The same law that had been used to legitimate and legalize European imperialism was reformed and embraced by the colonized subjects of European imperial states who came to recognize that sovereignty was ultimately a right of peoples and nations everywhere: something valuable and useful that they could claim for themselves by right. When European empires were dismantled in the mid-twentieth century, and the colonial administrators went home, their political and legal handiwork, colonial states, nevertheless remained in place and were taken over by the local people who acquired full rights of sovereignty within that imported framework (Jackson 1990: 82–108). Overarching imperial sovereignty was replaced by the local sovereignty of each former colony, or groupings or segments of such colonies, that acquired independence. That important event was normally marked by a ceremonial occasion, usually midnight on a certain date, when the imperial standard was lowered for the last time and the proud flag of the newly independent country was raised in its place.

After centuries of legitimacy and legality imperial sovereignty became unlawful. That is explicitly registered in various UN General Assembly Resolutions, such as Resolution 3103 (1973), which portrayed colonialism as nothing less than 'a crime'. It now takes an effort to remember that much less than a century ago Western imperialism was a global system that seemed destined to continue indefinitely.

This discussion may be summarized. When a government exercises supreme and exclusive authority over a foreign territory and its population, that government can be said to possess imperial sovereignty. A foreign territory is somebody else's homeland. Imperial sovereignty is thus an assertion of superiority by a foreign power and a rejection of an independent right to rule of an indigenous government or people, thereby imposing a dependent status on the territory and its population. That imposed condition of inferiority and dependency was at the root of the universal demand by colonized peoples for political independence on the grounds of their inherent right of self-determination on a basis of equality with everybody else who had it. That stage in the evolution of sovereignty, as well as several related stages, is discussed in the next chapter.

4

Popular Sovereignty

In the name of the people

Sovereignty began its historical voyage as the right of kings and other absolute rulers: 'I am your sovereign and I shall exercise authority over you, my subjects, in whatever way only I can decide.' Sovereignty would seem to end its journey as popular sovereignty: when the people are sovereign everybody is included in sovereignty and nobody is excluded. 'We the people are sovereign over ourselves. Nobody has any right to exercise the authority of the state against our will or without our consent.'

By 'popular sovereignty' I refer to the notion that the authority of the final word resides in the political will or consent of the people of an independent state. Thomas Paine expressed the idea in his political tract on 'the rights of man': 'The Nation is essentially the source of all sovereignty; nor can any individual, or any body of men, be entitled to any authority which is not expressly derived from it' (Oakeshott 1939: 20). This is a classic statement of the liberal doctrine of popular sovereignty. The idea, however, is anything but easy to pin down. The expression 'the people' is an abstraction, not a concrete reality. It is not 'the population', which is an empirical reference to an aggregation of individual persons. The people are most of those same persons considered as a political community. The American people, for example, are not all the residents of the United States, which includes many persons, such as myself, who are not Americans. The American people are all the members of the political community named the United States: its citizens. They are recognized by their constitution and symbolized by their flag, the stars and stripes, which conveys the idea of their nation: *E pluribus unum*: out of many, one.

Popular sovereignty is conspicuous in the political discourse of the United States which serves as a particularly significant historical instance of the idea. During his travels in America in the early nineteenth century Alexis de Tocqueville (1960, I: 58) observed: 'The American Revolution broke out, and the doctrine of the sovereignty of the people came out of the townships and took possession of the state . . . it became the law of laws.' It is evident in the two foundational documents of the republic: the Declaration of Independence (1776) and the Constitution (1787). Thomas Jefferson spoke of governments being 'instituted among men, deriving their just powers from the consent of the governed'. The preamble to the United States Constitution declares: 'We, the people of the United States, in order to form a more perfect Union . . . do ordain and establish this Constitution for the United States of America.' It was of course established by George Washington, James Madison, Alexander Hamilton, Benjamin Franklin, Gouverneur Morris and other 'founders' of the republic. The Bill of Rights enumerates rights of the people and declares that the powers not delegated to the United States 'are reserved to the States respectively, or to the people' (Art. X). In political and legal fact, however, the American people exist in virtue of their recognition by the Constitution and other fundamental laws of the United States and the institutions established by them.

We might be inclined to think the American people are a more substantial instance of popular sovereignty than most other peoples around the world. We probably would be correct, but only with important qualifications. During the dark moments of the American Civil War (1861–5) President Abraham Lincoln memorably proclaimed 'government of the people, by the people, for the people'. Since there was but one American constitution there also must be only one American people. The southern secessionists, the self-declared Confederate States of America, were dividing the people and in so doing were committing a traitorous and seditious action that must be suppressed, by armed force if necessary. The Confederacy, quite to the contrary, thought of themselves as states whose sovereignty was historically prior to the American constitution and had never been surrendered to it. They were referring to the original sovereignty of all states that were signatories to the constitution. That included not only South Carolina, Mississippi, Alabama, Virginia, and other southern states but also New York, Massachusetts, Pennsylvania, and indeed all American states, both north and south. That original sovereignty, they argued, was proclaimed by the Declaration of Independence, had been acknowledged in the 1783 treaty with Britain which formally concluded the revolutionary war, was articulated in Article X of the constitution, which itself was based on a 'law of compact' between those same sovereign states. It was Lincoln and the northern states that were breaking faith with the American constitution and its principle of the antecedent and continuing sovereignty of its constituent states.

These great struggles disclose typical perplexities of popular sovereignty. Who are the American people? Does a segment of the population have a right to assert a separate and subsequent declaration of independence? Can the American people be divided into two nations: the Confederacy and the Union? The historical answer, based on the outcome of the civil war, is that the American people are one and indivisible. That was of course an answer imposed by armed force. But that was consistent with the previous military action, the successful revolutionary war against Britain (1776–83), which vindicated the assertion of popular sovereignty in the American Declaration of Independence. In both their revolution and their civil war, as in so many other episodes of their emerging national life, Americans were anticipating struggles and conflicts of the nineteenth and twentieth centuries over the questions: Who are the people? Who has a valid claim to be a sovereign nation?

The people do not exist as such. They are formed, and sometimes they are forged, as in these American examples (Morgan 1988). The people themselves cannot constitute the state and govern the state. They cannot speak for themselves or by themselves. That is because they are not an entity or agent and they cannot exist or act on their own. The voice of the people—*vox populi*—must be invoked. The people must be recognized and organized by somebody in order to exist and to act. Democratic constitutions are instances of such recognition. Constitutions, however, are framed and enforced by only a relatively small segment of the population. Democratic elections are an organized means by which the people can express their political will and register their consent by casting their votes for political leaders and parties who solicit their support. Democratic elections, however, also are arranged and administered by certain people and not by the people. Referenda and plebiscites give voice to the people who respond to pre-selected and usually 'yes or no' questions written and placed before them by political elites. Politicians may listen to the voice of the people and even try to answer. They may speak and act on behalf of the people. They may regard the people as the final authority. The problem inherent in popular sovereignty still remains: the voice of the people must be invoked.

'The American people' is a quasi-religious refrain of anyone in the United States who wishes to speak with authority and be heard with attention (Morgan 1988). The American people can be called upon and spoken for but they cannot be criticized or reproached for they are without fault, rather in the same way that God cannot be criticized. 'The people are sovereign and can do no wrong' (Himmelfarb 1962: 142). The British journalist and writer G. K. Chesterton asked the question upon first arriving in the United States in the early twentieth century: 'What is America?' After his tour he gave the answer: it is 'a nation with the soul of a church' (Mead 1967: 262). Tocqueville made the same observation almost a century earlier: 'The people reign in the American political world as the Deity does in the universe. They are the cause and the aim of all things; everything comes from them, and everything is absorbed in them' (Tocqueville 1960, I: 60).

William Connolly (1987: 9) makes the point: 'Authority is an indispensable and dangerous practice.' That dilemma is nowhere more evident than in the practice of sovereign authority, which poses fundamental questions of answerability and accountability. Popes could be ignored and rendered superfluous when their authority was no longer accepted by those with power, particularly kings and other temporal rulers. Kings could be overturned, monarchy could be abolished, or royal authority could be emasculated and appropriated by parliaments. Parliaments could be elected by the people. Imperial sovereigns could be denounced and resisted by anti-imperial nationalists, if necessary by armed force. But how could the people be made accountable and answerable, and to whom? If the people must be constituted and organized by somebody, they can also be mobilized and even manipulated by somebody. They can even be deified, which may place extensive *de facto* authority in the hands of the deifiers. In the United States 'the people' is an expression that is employed by politicians and would-be politicians to lend unquestionable authority to their political platforms and policies.

A fundamental question arises at this point: how can the people be answerable and accountable if they are creatures and instruments of political elites? How are political elites kept in harness as servants of the people if the latter cannot act on their own, and if opinions can be put in their mouth by those same elites? This is the problem of populism. It is also the problem of totalitarian democracy, discussed later in this chapter. Similar questions were raised in the late eighteenth century by the American Federalists, who placed their political faith in civil liberties and constitutional constraints. Those answers proved to be only partly satisfactory. There are no entirely satisfactory answers of which I am aware, and the dilemma persists in the United States as elsewhere. Sovereign authority and power has to be in somebody's hands. It cannot be in the hands of everybody.

Here, then, is a major turn in the history we are investigating: popular sovereignty overturns the doctrine that final authority rests with an individual or an oligarchy or some other segment of the population of a country—or with a foreign power, as in the case of imperial sovereignty. That might seem to be the fulfilment of the destiny of state sovereignty and the end of its history. As indicated, however, the people have to be called into existence and kept in existence by somebody. That suggests that the notion of popular sovereignty is not as straightforward as it might seem to be; in fact, it is more tangled and knotted than the other ideas we have considered thus far.

Parliamentary sovereignty

Parliament is usually understood to be not only a legislative but also a representative body. The people in whole and in parts (constituencies, electoral districts, ridings, wards, etc.) are 'made present'—represented—in the legislature or national assembly by individuals elected from among the people. The parliamentarians govern on behalf of the people, who cannot govern themselves. The British parliament gave voice to the people in a significant way only when it became democratic in the nineteenth and early twentieth centuries, starting with the Reform Act of 1832 and culminating in the enfranchisement of women in 1928. Prior to that time the British parliament was geographically representative of landowners and certain boroughs across the country but the majority of the population were not represented. Even though the voice of the people was explicitly invoked from the beginning of the American revolution, the United States Congress was democratized belatedly, starting in the early nineteenth century but culminating only in the mid-twentieth century via desegregation and enfranchisement of African Americans, as legally required by the 1954 Supreme Court ruling in *Brown v. Board of Education* and the 1964 Federal Civil Rights Act.

British parliaments were called into existence and dissolved at the pleasure of the monarch. That was so even though a degree of parliamentary independence characterized the English political tradition and set it apart from the practices of many continental European countries before the nineteenth century. Members of parliament wrestled with the king for supreme state authority, but that was mostly a contest of rival groups of aristocrats—Whigs and Tories—seeking to influence the monarch or sideline the monarch and control the state directly. That centuries-long contention eventually came to an end in the triumph of 'parliamentary sovereignty': the doctrine that the politicians in parliament, acting collectively through their discussions, debates, and votes, have the final word in the state. Today British monarchs have very little constitutional authority: they have been politically neutered. Parliament is supreme.

Time and again in the literature it is pointed out that sovereignty has no constitutional limit. Initially it was the king who was understood to be unbound by any higher authority, except possibly God: royal absolutism. Later it was parliament that was seen as sovereign in that same legally unlimited way. The definitive statement of the British doctrine of parliamentary sovereignty is by A.V. Dicey (1956: xxxvi–xxxvii): 'Parliament has the right to make or unmake any law whatever ... no person or body is recognised ... as having a right to override or set aside the legislation of Parliament; the right or power of Parliament extends to every part of the King's dominions.' Parliamentary sovereignty is portrayed colourfully but also cogently in the often repeated example: if parliament decides that a dog is a person for certain legal purposes, then for those purposes a dog is indeed a person even though in every other respect a dog is a dog, either a pet or a working dog or a hunting dog or whatever else a dog can in fact be. That captures the notion of unlimited legislative competence: parliament 'can be challenged by no one and is not bound by its own decisions' (Scruton 1996: 441–2). What parliament decides is the law—until parliament decides differently, when that becomes the law.

If parliament were limited by some other authority, that person or institution or constitution would be sovereign. That clearly is the case of the United States Congress, which never held a monopoly of state authority the way the British parliament did after the overthrow of the Stuart dynasty in the late seventeenth century. The Senate and the House of Representatives hold power concurrently with the President and the Supreme Court in a constitutional system of checks and balances. That is in accordance with the doctrine of the division of powers nowhere better expressed than by James Madison in *The Federalist*, no. 51. Constitutional authority was also divided between the national government and state governments in a federal system. That is a basic constitutional difference between the United States and Britain. It is the Constitution that is sovereign and not the Congress—or the President or the Supreme Court or individual states of the Union. On closer inspection, however, it becomes apparent that the British parliament is also confined constitutionally in what it may do and how it may go about it. The constitutions of the United Kingdom and the United States are different but both countries operate a regime of constitutional government: a 'government of laws': the 'rule of law'.

That point has been developed with characteristic discernment by Ernest Barker (1963: 45). He notices that the root idea of parliament is captured in the word 'parley' which conveys the notion of meeting, conference, council, dialogue, discussion, negotiation, and the like. Parliaments are places where the leading politicians assemble to discuss and debate the most important political issues of the day prior to making a decision in a vote on proposed legislation. If a bill passes it becomes the law of the land. It is in parliament that Michael Oakeshott's (1991: 206) observation that 'politics has always been three-quarters talk' is most clearly evident. Parliamentary talk is not trivial or casual: it is not 'mere rhetoric'. Nor is it the abstract theoretical talk of academics. It is the practical and down-to-earth talk of politicians and their officials: it is politically, legally, and administratively consequential. The art of rhetoric is adroitness and forcefulness in parliamentary debates to persuade parliamentarians (and members of the public) of the desirability or necessity, wisdom or folly of proposed legislation—before the seal of parliamentary authority is stamped on it.

That is not the end of the matter, however. Barker (1963: 212–15) speaks of the legislature as the 'immediate sovereign' and the constitution of a state as 'the ultimate or normative sovereign'. A regime of parliamentary sovereignty cannot exist unless the parliamentarians operate in accordance with a body of agreed rules and procedures. Otherwise it would be impossible for them to arrive at a final word in an orderly way. There would always be a threat of anarchy and breakdown. There would be no parliament in fact and thus no parliamentary sovereignty. That happens in countries with little experience or tradition of parliamentary government, of which there are many around the world.

Barker carries the analysis one step farther by calling our attention to the way parliamentary discussion rests not only on the constitutional rules of the state but ultimately on the 'sovereignty of social thought' (1963: 214–15). That refers to normative ideas that parliamentarians employ in their discussions and debates to give their arguments greater cogency and legitimacy. He points to justice as a fundamental idea in this regard. It could equally be peace, security, liberty, equality, welfare, or other ideas of similar stature. This is the sovereignty of the political community's normative standards which are invoked in parliamentary discourse to sanctify proposed legislation: the 'national interest', the 'common good', the 'public interest', 'national security', 'civil rights', 'public welfare', etc. However vague or elastic these expressions may be in practice, they nevertheless serve as basic norms that parliamentarians invoke to sanction their policies or condemn those of their opponents. The people's interest, good, security, rights, welfare, etc. cannot be quarrelled with. Parliament, therefore, is a political place where the operative ideals of a political community can be expressed via discussion and debate and registered in legislation.

Of course, that is by assuming that parliamentarians are not the hostages of sectional interests or ideologies. If that were the case, parliament could still be the place where some measure of agreement is hammered out and made into law. It could not quite so readily be the place where the common good or the public welfare or some other norm or value of the political community is employed for crafting and assessing the laws. Instead, it is where parliamentarians are agents of special interests and lobbies. In that case 'the people' or 'the nation' are fractured and fragmented into so many divisions and splinters. It is that threat or temptation that Edmund Burke is rejecting in his famous remarks to the electors of Bristol (1777): 'Parliament is not a congress of ambassadors from different and hostile interests . . . but Parliament is a deliberative assembly of one nation, with one interest, that of the whole' (Hill 1975: 158).

This Platonic idea of parliamentarians as political guardians of the entire nation is easier said than done. It is activities of 'log-rolling' and 'horse-trading'—such as we see in the routine business of United States congressional committees—that more accurately characterizes the way in which the final word is registered in parliamentary regimes. In such places what we have is not a body of statesmen and stateswomen giving voice to the political community's norms prior to holding a vote that will determine the shape and substance of legislation. What we have are politicians organized into parties or factions to which they are answerable and for which they are fighting in parliamentary discussions and debates. The parliamentarians and parties might even be indebted to single-interest lobbies that contribute to their electoral campaigns in exchange for consideration and patronage, as happens whole-sale in the United States Congress. But even if this is a more accurate portrait of the legislative process, which it surely is, that process could not occur at all unless all parties could agree to parliamentary rules of the political game, in this instance the rule of majority decision-making. It is the author-ity of those rules which constitute the foundation of par-liamentary sovereignty—even where sectional and vested interests are powerful—as long as those rules are observed and not ignored by those who are subject to them.

Parliamentary representatives are supposed to give voice to the people or at least some of the people. Parliaments have always been understood in that way even when the people they represent are at most only a minority segment of the total population of a country, as was the case in Britain and the United States until well into the nineteenth century. That inti-mate connection between parliament and electorate is of course heightened when the electors of parliament multiply to include the entire adult population of a country, as happened in the nineteenth and twentieth centuries in most Western countries. It is when such a relation is established between a parliament and a universally enfranchised citizenry, when the former are not only conceived as representatives of the people but are elected by them, that we begin to think of parliament as expressing their collective will or consent: popular sovereignty. That relation between parliament and the people is normally understood as representative democracy.

Democratic sovereignty

Difference of opinion, disagreement, and controversy is inher-ent in political life. In a political controversy who shall have the final word? We have parliaments because we are determined to resolve our disagreements by discussion, debate, and voting rather than by war or rebellion. That is the doctrine of parliamentary sovereignty. The doctrine of popular sovereignty takes that reasoning a step farther by assigning the final word to the people, understood as both the source and the end of state authority. That doctrine is closely associated with the United States of America. It was evident to Tocqueville (1960, I: 57): 'If there is a country in the world where the doctrine of the sovereignty of the people . . . can be studied in its application to the affairs of society, and where its dangers and its advantages may be judged, that country is assuredly America.'

America, for Tocqueville, was popular sovereignty and democracy *par excellence*. But that seemingly straightforward idea is freighted with difficulties and ambiguities having to do not only with giving the people the final word but also with deciding who shall count as 'the people'. Before the people can exist a population must be formed into a unity or community. That issue is addressed later in the chapter. We should be aware of two distinctive and somewhat different ideas captured by the words 'democracy' and 'popular'. According to the *Oxford English Dictionary Online*, 'popular' primarily signifies 'the people as a whole as distinguished from any particular class'. But it also means 'the common people' as distinguished from people of high status, wealth, or power. The same ambiguity applies to the word 'democracy', which denotes both 'that form of government in which the sovereign power resides in the people as a whole' and 'that class of the people which has no hereditary or other special rank or privilege; the common people (in reference to their political power)'.

Hence, to say that a country is a 'democracy' could be a reference to constitutional authority in which the people as a whole are in some sense supreme, or it could refer to substantive policies which seek to maximize the power of the common people by placing the agencies and resources of the state at their service. The former notion is that of 'constitutional democracy', which involves 'the restraining of power under law' (Friedrich 1963: 198). In that conception democracy is a check on the abuse of power by the rulers: the liberal conception of democracy. The latter idea is that of 'peoples' democracy' which involves empowerment: expanding the power of the common people, as in the notion of 'worker's democracy', and giving it a policy direction dictated by their interests or concerns or wants or needs (Macpherson 1969). In that meaning, 'democracy' is a social movement that installs the common people as the political community. 'Peoples' democracy' is characteristic of socialist and particularly Marxist ideology: the people understood as a social class: the masses, the proletariat. It is obvious that the restrictive and selective notion of the people as a social class conflicts with the open and undifferentiating notion of the people as a whole political community. I shall confine my discussion in this section to the latter idea. I return to the restrictive notion in the next section.

Democracy, as a liberal idea, is a constitutional arrangement that gives the people as a whole the final word in the political affairs of their country. The people are a constitutional check on the power of the government and a validating source of their legitimacy. That is the prevailing notion of democracy, although by no means the only notion, that has taken root in Western countries. Liberal democracy is a form of constitution that vests sovereignty in the people defined as a citizenry with fundamental civil and political rights. That is the status of the people under the American constitution and other liberal democratic constitutions. Those rights are foundational: they are only to be set aside in extreme emergencies, such as times of war or civil insurrection. Even such exceptional measures, however, are qualified and circumscribed by law.

A constitutional democracy, then, is a regime of popular sovereignty based on citizenship, which could be either a direct democracy or a representative democracy. The oldest example of such a regime is direct democracy in which the citizens assemble in a certain place at a certain time to debate and decide issues affecting their common affairs: e.g. Athenian democracy. But direct democracy is scarcely suited for modern nation-states with sizeable territories and populations. We are reminded by a classical scholar that 'in a very large majority of the Greek city-states the adult male citizens numbered fewer than 10,000 and, in many, fewer than 5,000'

(Finley 1983: 59). The nearest modern approximation is probably New England 'town hall democracy'. But New England town halls cannot decide important questions affecting the common affairs of the American people or even the people of Massachusetts or Vermont. They can only decide local questions of their townships. The difference between democracy in ancient Athens and democracy in, say, Burlington, Vermont, is not the size of the cities—which are about the same. The difference lies in the political fact that ancient Athens was a state. When Athens was a democracy its citizen rulers had to face the challenges and exercise the responsibilities that come with independent statehood and statecraft: security, survival, war, peace, etc.

Most modern democracies have millions of citizens, and some of them have hundreds of millions. That sheer weight of numbers necessitates that democratic arrangements be indirect and representative. In a liberal democracy the people are constituted politically as an electorate based on universal suffrage. Representative democracy is a practical way of giving the people the final say in the political affairs of their country. The electorate are periodically canvassed in accordance with certain democratic procedures and practices: namely regular, free, and fair elections that are conclusive in deciding the question 'who shall rule?' Constitutional democracy can in that way express the sovereignty of the people.

But for some political philosophers democracy is supposed to give the people not only 'a voice' but also an 'actual part' in government. John Stuart Mill argued for popular sovereignty in the following terms:

> There is no difficulty in showing that the ideally best form of government is that in which the sovereignty, or supreme controlling power in the last resort, is vested in the entire aggregate of the community; every citizen not only having a voice in the exercise of that ultimate sovereignty, but being, at least occasionally, called on to take an actual part in the government, by the personal discharge of some public function, local or general. (Oakeshott 1939: 25)

The rule of the people is a tricky proposition, as Mill's tentative wording implies. Direct involvement of the population in the activity of governing modern nation-states is widely recognized as problematic and usually ill-advised. Some markers of political involvement are called for. Jack Lively (1975: 30) draws the following distinctions of declining degrees of popular rule: (1) that everybody should be personally involved in making law, determining policy, and administering the state; (2) that everybody should be personally involved in deciding general laws and policies; (3) that rulers should be accountable to the ruled; (4) that rulers should be accountable to the representatives of the ruled; (5) that rulers should be elected by the ruled; (6) that rulers should be elected by the representatives of the ruled; (7) that rulers should act in the interests of the ruled.

These distinctions can serve as a springboard to discuss the question of popular sovereignty in constitutional democracies. It is clear that 7 need not be democratic: it could indicate benevolent despotism or some other kind of paternalist government. It is obvious that 1 and 2 are unrealistic if not indeed utopian when applied to national government and not merely to small-scale local government. In large and populous states, which have become a political reality almost everywhere in the last century or two, the involvement of every citizen in decision-making could only be arranged by means of plebiscites or referenda, if it could be arranged at all. But such a canvassing of public choice grossly simplifies the political issue at stake by reducing it to one question (or a few questions) which must call for simple answers, usually either 'yes' or 'no'. Moreover, as noted above, referendum questions are written and placed before the voting people by political elites. Those elites, by being able to pose the questions, are the ones who constrain the answers or even shape the answers, in which case the final word resides with them.

The invention of personal computers and related technology and its widespread distribution among national populations does not overcome that difficulty. Technology is never a substitute for human decision-making; at best it is an aid. Suppose a populist arrangement for canvassing the people's decisions could be made to work, that is, the people could regularly and readily register the final word on important issues of law and policy, say by referenda conducted via the internet. That surely would be unwise if many of the people canvassed that way are in no position to decide on a reasonable and informed basis the important issue at stake. That defect is likely to be widespread even among the comparatively well-educated populations of Western democracies. If an uninformed or unreasonable majority routinely decided important questions of public law and policy, it might be a disaster for everybody. That, too, is generally recognized.

Representative democracy is intended to avoid such difficulties by giving the final word to the members of parliament or congress or the national assembly while keeping them ultimately beholden to the electorate. Their very role as elected representatives demands that they should be better informed and less arbitrary than the average citizen in dealing with issues of government law and policy. How can they manage to perform their role? It is not because they are any wiser than average citizens or superior in other ways. It is because their future political careers, to be decided at the next election, may depend on the consequences of their publicly stated opinions and actions. The citizens in representative democracies are not in a position to decide what the law or policy shall be. They are in a position to decide who from among the parties and politicians contesting for their votes shall be their representatives. That is their role.

To return to a point made earlier: the people in a representative democracy are creatures of the constitutional arrangements of the state; they do not and cannot exist on their own. There cannot be 'a people' in any meaningful political sense without a democratic constitution and institutional arrangements deriving from it which enfranchise and organize the population into a political community: citizenship, civil and political rights, electoral systems, political parties, free press, etc. The political arrangements of a representative democracy involve not only the electorate and their representatives but also the institutions by which they are all gathered into a democratic polity. Everybody of significance must be a democrat if representative democracy is to work. It fails to work in countries where political elites and their followers may claim to be democrats when seeking political offices but prove to be autocrats or oligarchs or dictators or tyrants when they get their hands on them. There are still many such countries around the world.

Representative democracy expresses the sovereignty of the people in the various ways identified by Jack Lively's gradations 3 to 6 which mark greater to lesser degrees of democratic accountability of the rulers to the ruled. Those are the arrangements that we commonly find in well-ordered democracies such as the United States, most countries of the European Union, Japan, Canada, Australia, New Zealand, and Israel among others. So, if this is what is meant by democratic sovereignty, it is clear that the final say on the part of the people is their right and opportunity to determine the outcome of democratic elections via the ballot box.

To sum up thus far: a people cannot exist in political reality without a constitution which validates their existence and which is widely if not indeed universally accepted. The clearest and most significant case in point is the United States, where the Constitution provides the basic vocabulary and grammar of political life. The Constitution is fundamental to the American way of talking politics and doing politics. The American people are the creatures of the United States Constitution and its late eighteenth-century framers. They cannot amend the Constitution, nor could they create it in the first place. But their role is absolutely fundamental to American democracy which could not exist and make sense without the people.

Totalitarian sovereignty

A doctrine of popular sovereignty was at the heart of French revolutionary discourse in the late eighteenth century. The constitution of 1791 declared: 'Sovereignty is one, indivisible, inalienable, and imprescriptible; it belongs to the Nation; no group can attribute sovereignty to itself nor can an individual arrogate it to himself.' Monarchy and Aristocracy were finished. The rule of the common people was underway. What the French revolutionaries succeeded in doing, however, was 'attributing' and 'arrogating' sovereignty to themselves in the name of 'the people'. France ended up with the first modern dictator: Napoleon Bonaparte (Cobban 1939: 79). That has been portrayed as 'totalitarian democracy' (Talmon 1970: 43–8) which is not only a Fascist or Communist doctrine of the twentieth century but a much earlier political programme that dates back to late eighteenth-century France.

If popular sovereignty is taken literally, if the people are to be as 'sovereign' as absolutist kings and dynasties were sovereign, there will be problems in conceiving of it and arranging it. How can a national population be politically unified to the extent that they could act like one sovereign ruler or ruling elite rather than a multitude of individuals? That problem was posed by French intellectuals in the eighteenth century in the period leading up to the revolution of 1789. They wanted to take sovereignty away from absolute monarchs and give it to the mass of the population to whom they believed it properly belonged.

The French philosopher Jean Jacques Rousseau pondered the problem of making the people absolutely sovereign and came up with a theoretical solution that turned out to be one of the most famous arguments of modern political theory. He believed that the people could act in unison by agreeing to respect absolutely their 'common interest' to which he gave the name 'the general will' (Rousseau 1988: 200–2). Sovereignty was 'nothing less than the exercise of the general will'. By obeying the general will, and setting aside their own personal, parochial, or sectional interests, the people would be able to rule in the manner of a sovereign. Rousseau's argument presupposes the ability of everybody to recognize the general will and not to mistake it for their own self-interest or some other interest, and it presupposes their inclination to faithfully obey it and carry it out in their own conduct. Every member of the nation would be in political communion with every other member of the nation. The population would accordingly do not what is best only for themselves or their families or their towns or cities or class or caste, but what is best for the nation as a whole: 'the nation is not the aggregate of men, women and children but a confraternity of faith' (Talmon 1970: 234).

According to J. L. Talmon (1970: 46–7), 'Rousseau demonstrates clearly the close relation between popular sovereignty taken to the extreme, and totalitarianism.' That patently was not what Rousseau was seeking to bring about. He was searching for an irrefutable argument to justify sovereignty resting in 'the consent of the [whole] people' (Rousseau 1988: 201).

He was trying to show how sovereign authority could conceivably reside in the hands of the entire political community. Totalitarian control, in the name of the common people, was the state of affairs that the most determined power seekers of the French Revolution tried to bring about. They adopted and twisted Rousseau's ideas to serve their own political ends. They imposed their will on the population in the name of the common people. The only way that could be arranged was by wholesale destruction of the monarchy, and its aristocratic supporters, and by replacing that old regime with a new centralized apparatus of power exclusively controlled by those same revolutionaries, exercised in the name of the common people but used to intimidate and even terrorize them. The word 'terrorism' was coined at that time (*OED*).

The name of 'the people' can be used to absolve or mask the abuse of political power on a grand scale. In revolutionary France, popular sovereignty became the justification of a centralized, powerful, arbitrary, intolerant regime. Alexis de Tocqueville (1955: xi) summarizes his famous argument on how the French Revolution turned into a despotism, in which the people became the slaves of the revolutionary elites rather than their masters:

> I shall show how a government, both stronger and far more autocratic than the one which the Revolution had overthrown, centralized once more the entire administration, made itself all-powerful, suppressed our dearly bought liberties, and replaced them by a mere pretence of freedom; how the so-called 'sovereignty of the people' came to be based on the votes of an electorate that was neither given adequate information nor an opportunity of getting together and deciding on one policy rather than another; and how the much vaunted 'free vote' in matters of taxation came to signify no more than the meaningless assent of assemblies tamed to servility and silence. Thus the nation was deprived both of the means of self-government and of the chief guarantee of its rights, that is to say the freedom of speech, thought, and literature which ranked among the most valuable and noblest achievements of the Revolution.

Tocqueville is noting how difficult the effort to institute the literal 'sovereignty of the people' can prove to be in reality, how easily it can be exploited by ruthless true believers or corrupted by power-hungry cynics, as happened not only in the French Revolution but in revolutions that followed, including the Russian Revolution of 1917, the Chinese Revolution of 1949, and less consequential revolutions in Europe, Asia, Africa, and Latin America. The popular sovereign turned out to be a dictator: Napoleon in France, Lenin and Stalin in Russia, Mao in China, among others. The population ended up in a position far closer to servility than sovereignty: the subservient instrumentality of the political will of the revolutionary leader and his regime.

The notion of popular sovereignty has always been a standing invitation to anyone who wishes to take advantage of it. The population or at least segments of the population cannot be immune to guile and deception, threat or temptation, from individuals and factions who are determined to exploit the idea of the people for their own ends. The population can in the right circumstances be manipulated. They can be deceived and manoeuvred. Some among them can be persuaded or tempted or conned or threatened into performing undemocratic, uncivil, unconstitutional, unlawful, or other activities hostile to democracy. They can be divided and reduced to pliant quietude. In the name of 'the people', as in the name of God, monstrous acts can be threatened and carried out.

The sovereignty of the people understood in the literal sense as a government in which the masses actually have the final word that cannot be overridden because it is 'sovereign'—that proposition turns out to be a myth and a dangerous doctrine indeed (James 1989). When it is promoted with ruthlessness the end result can be a totalitarian dictator who seizes power and exercises mastery over the whole people, even seeking to remake the people in the image of the totalitarian dictatorship. The Italian Fascist dictator Benito Mussolini put it well: 'The Fascist State, the highest and most powerful form of personality, is a force, but a spiritual force, which takes over all the forms of the moral and intellectual life of man ... It wants to remake, not the forms of human life, but its content, man, character, faith. And to this end it requires discipline and authority that can enter in the spirits of men and there govern unopposed' (Oakeshott 1939: 168). The whip hand of the Fascist state or the Nazi state or the Communist state is greater, indeed incomparably greater, than that of any absolute monarch.

Here the state is conceived not to reflect and respond to the popular will—as in free and fair elections in constitutional democracies—but rather to dictate it and enforce it with total command and unrelenting determination. The dictator and his regime treat law as the expression of their will to totalitarian power. When the population come to realize their exposure to an arbitrary and ruthless dictatorship, they understandably become pliant and subservient. They keep their heads down, toe the line, and avoid drawing any attention to themselves, in full awareness that otherwise they could easily become targets of the wrath of the totalitarian regime and its willing enforcers and executioners. That exploited and twisted notion of popular sovereignty is associated with the most devastating human episodes the modern world has yet had to witness and endure, namely the totalitarian dictatorships of the twentieth century and the large-scale wars they spawned, particularly the Second World War. The fact that far greater repression has been imposed in the name of the people than was ever imposed in the name of the king or the dynasty is one of the greatest ironies in the evolution of the idea.

National self-determination

The French revolutionary doctrine of a unified nation-state established a precedent for political developments in Europe in the nineteenth and twentieth centuries. That was evident in the mobilization of various European nationalities—defined by language—to form their own sovereign state: the Italians, the Germans, the Greeks, the Bulgarians, etc. The Italians and the Germans each consolidated several smaller sovereign jurisdictions into a larger Italy and a greater Germany in the 1860s and early 1870s. The Greeks (1830) and the Bulgarians (1908) each broke away from an imperial and multinational state, the Turk-centred Ottoman Empire, and formed their own independent nation-state.

Among the most instructive instances of national unification was Germany which historically had been a people divided among dynastic sovereignties, imperial cities, and various other territorial jurisdictions—as indicated in chapter 3. In the mirror of nineteenth century nationalism, those pre-existing sovereignties were standing in the way of the overdue birth of a German nation-state. Those old jurisdictions would have to give up their sovereignty, which would be transferred to a united Germany. Also standing in the way were international borders behind which German minority populations were trapped in neighbouring countries. Germans living in Denmark and France would have to be liberated—not by allowing them to move freely across the border but by German armies conquering and annexing the Danish and French territories on which their homes were located. That militarist unification of the German people was carried out by Chancellor Otto von Bismarck in the 1860s and early 1870s.

All states have populations but not every state has a people. This 'problem' of making the state territorial shoe fit the national language foot was addressed by John Stuart Mill in the mid-nineteenth century. He argued that an independent state should contain only one nation, and if it contained more than one it would face destabilizing and disintegrating pressures: 'Free institutions are next to impossible in a country made up of different nationalities' (Mill 2000: 393). That was also the official British view in colonial Canada after the conquest of Quebec in 1759, which contained not only an original French-speaking population but now an immigrant English-speaking population as well. Rebellions occurred in Canada in 1837. The British imperial government in London asked John George Lambton, first Earl of Durham, to investigate and report on the problem. His proposed solution (never carried out) was assimilation:

> I found two nations warring in the bosom of a single state . . . I perceived that it would be idle to attempt any amelioration of laws or institutions until we could first succeed in terminating the deadly animosity that now separates the inhabitants of Lower Canada into the hostile divisions of French and English . . . it must henceforth be the first and steady purpose of the British Government to establish an English population, with English laws and language . . . and to trust its government to none but a decidedly English legislature. (Durham 1839)

The doctrine that a people and a territory should coincide within a single independent state became widely accepted in Europe and America. Historically significant instances of this change are the national states that emerged in Eastern Europe at the end of the First World War out of the disintegration or dismantling of the German, the Russian, and above all the Austro-Hungarian and the Turkish empires. Austria, Hungary, Poland, Czechoslovakia, Yugoslavia, Lithuania, Latvia, Estonia, and Finland arose from the shattered remains of those empires. In his famous 'Fourteen Points' speech (1918) President Woodrow Wilson made it a primary consideration in the design and construction of new states. 'What we demand in this war . . . is that the world be made fit and safe to live in; and particularly that it be made safe for every peace-loving nation which, like our own, wishes to live its own life, determine its own institutions.'

If the alignment of people and territory were a relatively straightforward question of social engineering the story might end there. But that is not the case. That can come as no surprise after a moment's reflection on the relationship between people and territory, which is usually an awkward fit even under the best circumstances. The practical problem of determining who shall count as comprising the people is anything but easy to solve. If it is clear who are the people the problem still remains that territory and people are not usually aligned closely and comfortably. It is often problematical, both politically and morally, either to redraw territorial borders or to relocate populations in an effort to achieve alignment. The first raises questions of partition or secession, the second questions of forced population transfer or what has come to be called ethnic cleansing (Jackson Preece 1998c). The difficulty and in many cases the impossibility of alignment is one of the major lessons not only of attempts to create new national states at the end of the First World War, but also of territorial partitions and population transfers during and after the Second World War and more recently (Schechtman 1946; Henckaerts 1995). The period from 1939 to 1949 has come to be known as the 'black decade' of Central European history when not only the Nazis during the Second World War but also the allied powers immediately afterwards engaged in massive acts of coerced and forced migration (Stola 1992).

That episode involved far-reaching realignment of national boundaries, particularly those of Poland and Germany.

When the people or the nation, rather than the ruler or the government, become the referent for sovereignty, the issue of national minorities arises at the same time (Jackson Preece 1998a). Point 12 in President Wilson's speech acknowledged that post-war Turkey should be 'assured a secure sovereignty', but 'the other nationalities which are now under Turkish rule should be assured an undoubted security of life and an absolutely unmolested opportunity of autonomous development.' As it happened, they were recognized as sovereign states. However, it proved impossible to draw borders that neatly contained national populations within their own nation-state and without any remnants left outside. Most states had foreign minorities: Hungary ended up with a Slovak minority, Romania had a Hungarian minority, Czechoslovakia had Hungarian and German minorities, etc. In short, the desire to redraw international boundaries to create nation-states almost inevitably engenders dislocated peoples, such as national minorities, no matter how carefully or scientifically the map is drawn.

The issue of national minorities alerts us to difficulties involved with national self-determination in a political world organized on a territorial basis of state sovereignty. The territory and the people are not neatly aligned in most cases. Most independent countries contain several territorially differentiated peoples, and some contain many. Who are the self-determining people and where is their sovereign territory? That question can be asked about many peoples and territories. Consider just one example: the case of Northern Ireland (Ulster), an enclave of British sovereignty in the north-east corner of the island we refer to as Ireland. There is no question that Northern Ireland is territory that belongs to the United Kingdom. And there is no question that the rest of the island belongs to the Irish Republic. There is some uncertainty, however, as to who are 'the people' in Northern Ireland, which contains both a Protestant majority population (mostly British-loyalist), and a Catholic minority population (mostly Irish-nationalist). If Ulster remains under British sovereignty and the Catholic population remains where it is, there will be a Catholic minority. If it is unified with the Irish Republic and the Protestant population remains where it is, there will be a larger Protestant minority in the republic. The minority fact will not be erased merely by transferring sovereignty over Northern Ireland from Britain to Ireland.

Various 'solutions' to such 'problems' have been attempted or proposed. As we have seen, one policy is assimilation, which pursues the ideal of a unified nation-state by identifying the required language (or religion or other national marker) and excluding as far as possible all others. The 'melting pot' by which immigrants from continental European countries were formed into English-speaking Americans, or at least their children were moulded into that identity, is similar.

Policies that pursue a solution either by partitioning territory or by relocating people are much harsher. Ireland was partitioned between North and South in 1921 and repercussions involving periodical terrorist bombing and killing were still being experienced at the end of the twentieth century. The same can be said, even more emphatically, of the partition of British India (1947) and the partition of Palestine (1948), both of which involved religious definitions of the people. They also resulted in wars that attempted to redraw international borders yet again. Israel fought several wars that altered borders with neighbouring Arab states to make Israelis more secure. For their part, the Arabs refused to accept as legitimate and lawful not only the borders but even the territorial existence of Israel. Pakistan subsequently experienced armed secession by the ethnically distinctive Bengali population of East Pakistan, who managed to seize sovereign statehood on that territory in the name of Bangladesh. What originally was a multicultural British India was now three independent successor states differentiated to a significant degree by either religion or ethnicity which defined 'the people' in each case.

Territorial partition or secession—the separation of a territory from an existing sovereign state—is frequently accompanied by massive population transfers, strikingly evident in the partition of British India, which drove millions of Indian Muslims to seek refuge in Pakistan, and millions of Pakistani Hindus to seek the same in India. They passed each other in endless lines, slogging on foot or riding in ox-carts with all their worldly goods, moving in opposite directions along the same roads and tracks toward the security and affinity of their own theocratic nation. At the end of the Second World War the borders of Eastern Europe were realigned by the victorious allied powers on the demand of Stalin. Those of Poland were relocated a significant distance westward, as if a giant had picked up the country and moved it. The Soviet Union thereby acquired new territory at Poland's expense, and Poland in turn acquired new territory at Germany's expense. Those border realignments also involved forced population transfer westward of millions of Poles and Germans, who had to pack up and move to remain in their native country. Today that would be ethnic cleansing—a violation of international human rights—which is no longer supposed to happen (Henckaerts 1995).

The Balkan wars of the 1990s, brought about by the disintegration of the Federal Republic of Yugoslavia, involved massive ethnic cleansing of people who did not fit the religious-nationalist profile of the emerging nation-states, particularly Orthodox Christian Serbia and Catholic Christian Croatia. Subsequent armed intervention by NATO to restore peace could not entirely reverse those ethnic cleansing for nation-building campaigns. These are among the most extreme recent instances of an uncompromising demand that the territory and the people must coincide, and that coercion and force may be used to relocate populations to make them coincide. In the foregoing examples, and others that could be referenced, there is more than an echo of the wars of religion of early-modern Europe, in which armed force was used to align sovereign borders with Catholic or Protestant confessions.

More accommodating and peaceful arrangements for distinctive peoples of sovereign states—federalism, bilingualism, multiculturalism, and the like—have become the practice in some countries. They all imply a somewhat different political universe in which the territory and the people are no longer as tightly and exclusively integrated as the doctrine of national self-determination presupposes. Canada, the United States, Belgium, Switzerland, and Australia give an indication of what such a world might look like if it became a more widespread reality.

Canada, for example, has officially recognized sub-national communities of its linguistically, culturally, and racially diverse population. Since its founding in the nineteenth century that country has rejected assimilation and melting-pot doctrines. Instead, Canada accommodated linguistic dualism—English and French—within a constitutional framework of federalism. The country became officially bilingual in 1967. The Canadian Charter of Rights and Freedoms (1982) affirms 'the preservation and enhancement of the multicultural heritage of Canadians' (section 27). The aboriginal people of Canada, the Indians, are officially recognized as 'first nations'. Today the country celebrates its multicultural diversity (Kenerman and Resnick 2005, Jackson Preece 2005, 1998b). Yet the doctrine of a nation-state still flourishes in some quarters. The French-speaking majority population of the province of Quebec have supported a nationalist or 'sovereigntist' Parti Québecois, which has campaigned for an independent, francophone Quebec. Even in a comfortable and relatively tolerant country like Canada, at least for some of its population, nationalism dies hard.

The lesson of the Canadian experience to date is that multinational self-determination within a single sovereign territory is workable. A threat of Quebec secession still remains, however. If that were to happen it would result not only in two independent countries side-by-side, but also very likely in substantial population transfers across the new international borders, although they would not be coerced or forced in any significant way. At the end of such a still hypothetical episode both Canada and Quebec would contain substantial minority populations. The main difference would be: francophone speakers living in Quebec would be a national majority and no longer a national minority.

The argument of this chapter raises a question concerning the future of state sovereignty in a world in which democratic ideas are circulating ever more widely among diverse population groupings of territorial states whose borders are fixed in their current location. The experience of a country like Canada may be suggestive of a future of the sovereign state in which international borders remain frozen in place, national assimilation or the population 'melting pot' is not pursued, yet national disintegration is avoided, and the state seeks to accommodate the diverse sub-national population groupings of domestic society by constitutional and administrative means which are recognizably democratic.

These are basically efforts to legitimize the sovereignty of the territorial state in the eyes of its multicultural domestic society. The question arises in an era, such as our own, when previously 'outsider' population groupings no longer are prepared to live in silence, sometimes under legal liabilities and constraints, as they were prepared to do in early-modern European states, in the settler states Europeans constructed in the Americas and elsewhere, and in European overseas empires and their successor Asian, African, and Middle Eastern states. This issue of the legitimacy of sovereign states in the eyes of diverse domestic population groupings that have awakened to public life can be expected to be at the forefront of both government attention and scholarly interest in the years to come.

Territorial sovereignty

Do a people or nation determine the territorial extent of their sovereign jurisdiction, or do bordered territorial jurisdictions define and delimit the sovereignty of peoples or nations? The doctrine of national self-determination prescribes the former, but the latter situation is closer to historical reality. Viewed historically, peoples or nations that shape territory in accordance with the doctrine of popular sovereignty are an exception rather than a commonplace. The received practice is to vest sovereignty in a bordered territory rather than a distinctive people or nation. Sovereignty is a territorial definition of political authority. Territoriality became the foundation principle of sovereign statehood in the early-modern period, and it has remained so ever since. It has been the given or starting point in response to which issues surrounding the people or the nation arise.

At the start of modern European history, sovereign rulers and dynasties were preoccupied with territory but were largely indifferent to the peoples that occupied it, providing they accepted their authority—and (in certain instances) conformed to their religion, as reflected in the royalist doctrine *cujus regio, ejus religio*. Later, during the era of nationalism, many sovereign governments became determined to ensure that the population spoke the national language and in other ways became part of the nation. When Germany conquered French-speaking Alsace in the Franco-Prussian War (1870–1) the new German authority in that area set about to ensure that the German language was taught in schools and used in other public institutions and places, so that Alsace would be integrated into the fatherland. When France reacquired sovereignty over the area at the end of the First World War, French was restored to its former position in the territory.

There have of course been itinerant and territory-occupying peoples in the modern era, indeed vast movements of them, most involved with Western imperialism. European colonists and settlers overran and took possession of the lands of Native North and South Americans, Aboriginal Australians, New Zealand Maoris, and indigenous peoples in other parts of the non-European world. They settled in very large numbers in the Americas, which drove the native inhabitants into the territorial margins and sometimes into virtual invisibility. Occasionally native inhabitants were wiped out. The European settlements defined the political map. Many of these settler countries, but particularly the United States, later could readily be shaped and justified in accordance with the doctrine of popular sovereignty, 'the people' being the colonial settlers and their descendants. It is no accident that the doctrine was enthusiastically taken up and given historically unprecedented significance by the American revolutionists. Their ancestors had come into the 'new world' and taken full possession of it. Their descendants were shaping it in accordance with ideas of themselves as a nation or people. Indigenous peoples were irrelevant.

Most European penetration, occupation, and control of territory in Asia, Africa, the Middle East, and other such places was, however, carried out by official or officially sanctioned representatives or agents of imperial states, or—as was often the case too—by armed merchants and traders operating under their licence and flag. Imperialism in these territories was an extension of European state sovereignty in the form not of settlement but of territorial control for reasons of state. These imperial territories were not new havens or homes overseas for disaffected or devoted or restless or ambitious people. They were not settler states that would one day perhaps become new European nations overseas comparable to the United States, the Latin American states, Canada, Australia, New Zealand, and for a time white South Africa. They were narrower and more utilitarian enterprises. They were new economic fields for exploitation or new strategic locations for military bases. The number of Europeans on the ground in most of these territories was relatively small in comparison with settled colonies.

These European overseas territories were from the beginning divorced from any idea of popular sovereignty, and that divorce had a long-term consequence. That was the eventual independence of territories which had been expediently acquired to serve imperial interests, and whose resident indigenous populations had been mobilized for those purposes. Those populations were rarely, if ever, conceived as a people or nation, either actual or potential, that would qualify for self-determination some day. The independent states that eventually emerged from decolonization in Asia, Africa, the Middle East, and other such places usually contained polyglot peoples that were deeply divided along religious, ethnic, linguistic, cultural, and other such lines. That, of course, is to read it from the sociological and self-determination angle. From an older perspective, these were typical sovereign territories of conquered or otherwise subdued and subjected populations—conglomerate or composite states—that would be familiar to most European rulers who lived before the age of nationalism (Elliott 1992, Gustafsson 1998).

In the mid-twentieth century the 'self' in self-determination was juridical and territory-focused more often that it was sociological and people-focused. The population conditions did not usually favour popular sovereignty. Exactly the opposite. Ernest Gellner (1993: 74) notes that in the fewer than 200 sovereign states of the contemporary world, 8,000 languages are spoken. Even if those languages are mostly local and minor, there are still very many more languages spoken by sizeable populations than there are sovereign states. Most states are linguistically divided. As indicated, the new states that were created or resurrected (Poland) in Eastern Europe at the end of the First World War had multinational populations. Most of the new state jurisdictions of ex-colonial Asia, Africa, and the Middle East contain several and often many linguistically or ethnically distinctive population groupings. The sociological or anthropological peoples of those places were not usually recognized as valid candidates for self-determination and self-government. The impractical and unviable proposition of a thousand sovereign states or more is readily apparent. It would require an overarching, world sovereign, which would involve the dissolution of existing sovereign states or their reduction into provinces or American-style 'states'. Those peoples mostly remain submerged beneath or divided between the borders of existing state jurisdictions.

In the world that emerged out of the disintegration or dismantling of Western empires in those areas neither nationality nor any other exclusively sociological definition of the political self was a valid basis for a claim to state sovereignty. The colonial territory whose borders were defined by the European imperialists, rather than the culturally distinct population groupings that were enclosed or divided by them, became the basis of the new sovereign state almost everywhere outside the Western world. That situation has persisted to the present day.

In the twentieth century the political map of the world became frozen in a territorial pattern shaped by borders established in the non-Western world by European imperial powers. Even though the territorial shoe did not come anywhere near to fitting the population foot in the greater number of cases, the prospect of changing the shoe was more daunting and disturbing than the problems of retaining it. That was particularly so when viewed from an international angle. Those inherited borders became sacrosanct and border change correspondingly difficult. The right of territorial conquest was extinguished along with the right of colonization. The practice of territorial partition was almost universally regarded with misgivings, no doubt owing to the violent troubles surrounding the Irish, Indian, and Palestine partitions in particular. Threats or acts of secession and irredentism were similarly treated with suspicion and were universally opposed.

International law sanctified all sovereign state boundaries regardless of population awkwardness or ill-fit in many cases. The League of Nations Covenant undertook 'to protect and preserve . . . the territorial integrity and existing political independence of all Members' (Art. 10). The League's system of guarantees for national minorities in Eastern Europe reflected that same territorial integrity doctrine. Minority recognition was less disruptive than border revision. Territories had to be stabilized. That was evident in the conclusions of a Commission of Jurists appointed by the League to examine the secessionist demands of Swedish residents of the Åland Islands, located in the Baltic Sea between Sweden and Finland, which became part of the new state of Finland at the end of the First World War. The Commission declared that 'international law does not recognize the right of national groups . . . to separate themselves from the State of which they form a part by the simple expression of a wish.'

The League of Nations eventually ceased to exist but Article 2 of the United Nations Charter upheld the same conservative territorial principle using almost identical language. The 1960 UN General Assembly 'Declaration on the Granting of Independence to Colonial Countries and Peoples' proclaimed that 'all peoples have the right of self-determination' but added the pointed qualifier that 'any attempt aimed at the partial or total disruption of the national unity or territorial integrity of a country is incompatible with the purposes and principles of the Charter of the United Nations.' Respect for borders was a sacred norm for the 1963 Organization of African Unity, and is the same for its successor, the African Union. The 1975 Helsinki Final Act expressed the principle that 'frontiers can [only] be changed, in accordance with international law, by peaceful means and by agreement.' The 1990 Charter of Paris for a New Europe reiterated the same principle. It was also the basis of the Dayton Agreement (1995) signed between Bosnia-Herzegovina, Croatia, and Serbia. The two key articles read as follows:

> The parties . . . shall fully respect the sovereign equality of one another . . . and shall refrain from any action, by threat or use of force or otherwise, against the territorial integrity or political independence of Bosnia and Herzegovina or any other state. (Article I)

> The Federal Republic of Yugoslavia and the Republic of Bosnia and Herzegovina recognize each other as sovereign independent States within their international borders. (Article X)

The territorial status quo has been preserved almost without exception even in the face of armed challenges. In Europe the major apparent exception is the unification of East and West Germany. It should be noted, however, that the external post-1945 borders of former East Germany and West Germany were not altered in the slightest degree by reunification. If Germans residing beyond these borders wanted to live in the new Germany they would have to pack up and move there. German territory would not be extended to include them. Bismarck was dead. The age of European-style nation-building was over.

It might be thought that the new states that emerged after the Cold War in the territories of the former Soviet Union and the former Yugoslavia contradict the territorial status quo practice. Weren't the various peoples involved—such as Ukrainians in the former Soviet Union and Croatians in former Yugoslavia—trying to create nineteenth century, European-style nation-states? Maybe they were. The fact remains, however, that the external and internal borders of each of those pre-existing federations were used to define the territorial jurisdiction of the successor sovereign states. The new borders were subsequently upheld even in the face of armed efforts to change them: for example, in Croatia, Bosnia, Serbia (Kosovo), and Russia (Chechnya). In Bosnia, the attempt by Serb militias to carve out territories by force, along ethno-religious lines, to create a Greater Serbia, was widely opposed and finally stopped by NATO intervention of 1995. In Kosovo, part of the territorial jurisdiction of what is now Serbia, the attempt by the Serbian government to cleanse its newly sovereign territory of a resident Albanian Moslem population with the same aim, was also stopped by NATO intervention in 1999.

Even in the Middle East the colonial frontiers which divided the Arab 'nation' into so many territorial jurisdictions are considered lawful and legitimate by the vast majority of ex-colonial Arab states. It seems nowadays that boundaries cannot be revised even to punish an aggressor state. Iraq retained its identical borders despite having suffered an overwhelming military defeat in the Gulf War of 1991. 'No-fly' zones established in Iraq by the United States and several other Western powers to protect the Kurdish population following the end of hostilities acknowledged the territorial integrity of Iraq. Proposals made by one or two United States Senators following the 2003 American and British occupation of Iraq, namely that its territory should be partitioned into separate states along the residential lines of its major Shiite, Sunni, and Kurdish populations, secured almost no international support, and none from states in the region.

We are living at a time when existing territorial jurisdictions are vested with exceptional international validity. The principle involved is that of *uti possidetis juris* ('as you have, so may you hold') according to which existing boundaries are the pre-emptive basis for determining territorial jurisdictions in the absence of mutual agreement of all affected state parties to do otherwise (Ratner 1996, Shaw 1996). The principle seeks to uphold the territorial integrity of states by demanding respect for existing borders unless all states who share them consent to change them. If consent is not forthcoming and change must occur, as in the violent disintegration of Yugoslavia, then the external border of the former state shall remain in place and internal borders shall be used to delineate the international boundaries of the successor sovereign states. That is the established norm for determining international boundaries in ex-colonial situations and in the break-up of states.

In 1991 a European Union Conference on Yugoslavia created an Arbitral Commission chaired by Robert Badinter, President of the French Constitutional Council, to rule on the validity of various claims for political independence in the sovereign territory of the Federal Republic of Yugoslavia and to determine whether these were acts of secession. The Commission made reference to the conditions that define a sovereign state: a delimited and demarcated territory, with a resident population, which was subject to an organized political authority that was independent. They noted that most component political units of Yugoslavia (Slovenia, Croatia, Macedonia, and Bosnia-Herzegovina) had asserted their independence, that the Yugoslavia authorities were unable to prevent these events, that the federal organs of Yugoslavia were no longer operating, and that 'the former national territory and population . . . are now entirely under the sovereign authority of the new states.' They judged that no Yugoslav state any longer existed. And they concluded that Yugoslavia was in the process of dissolution rather than in a secessionist conflict. Secession would under most circumstances be contrary to international law which affirms the territorial integrity of sovereign states, but state dissolution under circumstances of civil war is not a violation of international law (Pellet 1982, Ratner 1996).

The Commission made it clear that the dissolution was occurring along the lines of what had been the internal borders of the former Yugoslavia, which had become the international boundaries of the new successor states. That was in spite of the fact that those same borders did not neatly encapsulate the national population groups of former Yugoslavia—principally Serbs (Orthodox Christians), Croats (Catholics), and Moslems—but in fact divided them. There was no basis in international law for justifying any attempt to redraw those borders with the aim of unifying those divided population groups inside their own national states. In determining the validity of these new international borders the Commission underlined the vital importance of *uti possidetis juris*: 'The territorial integrity of States, this great principle of peace, indispensable to international stability . . . has today acquired the character of a universal and pre-emptory norm' (Pellet 1982: 178–85). National minorities did not possess a prima facie right of secession.

That statement captures the main justification associated with territorial sovereignty in the present-day world. That justification embodies two fundamental values held by the vast majority of sovereign governments nowadays. The first value, and the must fundamental, is the high realist premium they place on international order, and their evident willingness to sacrifice the right of national self-determination of particular peoples or nationalities for the sake of that overriding, prudential goal. The second is their Burkean regard for the certainty and stability of international law, and their very great reluctance to tamper with it, even in the face of localized disruptions and difficulties such as those noted above, and many others one could point to. That includes their profound scepticism regarding proposals for the partition of allegedly unviable states, as well as their opposition to secessionist and irredentist demands. The international system or society of sovereign states, it bears repeating, is a conservative club when it comes to territorial divisions and borders.

The end of sovereignty?

This brings me to the final point of the chapter, and one that recurs throughout the book: if historical experience is anything to go by, it suggests that the idea of sovereignty and the institutions associated with it will continue to evolve in ways that are not predictable. Teleological conceptions that postulate an end or terminus of that evolution warrant our scepticism. In sixteenth- and seventeenth-century Europe the terminus was the godly Christian state, either Protestant or Catholic, under a divinely appointed king. In eighteenth- and nineteenth-century Britain the terminus was the representative, sovereign parliament. In eighteenth-century America and France the terminus was the sovereign Republic and its people. In nineteenth- and twentieth-century Europe the terminus was the sovereign nation-state defined as a good fit between a language foot and a territorial shoe. In nineteenth- and twentieth-century America the terminus was the assimilation or at least integration of a racially and ethnically diverse population into one democratic nation or people. In the nineteenth and early twentieth centuries the terminus was national states in the Western world and Western imperialism in the rest of the world. In twentieth-century Asia and Africa the terminus was the territorially sovereign, ex-colonial state. In the late twentieth and early twenty-first centuries in some Western countries the terminus is starting to look like a democratic multicultural society.

That suggests that there is no teleological terminus, no determinate and final destination, and no 'end of history' in the evolution of sovereignty. There are merely variations and stages of the same basic theme which occur in different places at different times. State sovereignty will come to an end when people are no longer prepared to underwrite the doctrine that every political community must possess a government that is both superior to all other authorities in the country, and independent of all foreign governments. At some time in the future, probably later rather than sooner, state sovereignty will be abandoned and replaced by a different arrangement of political and legal authority on the planet. When that global transformation might be expected to occur and what could be expected to take its place is impossible to say. But there is no end in sight early in the twenty-first century.

5
Sovereignty and Humanity

Protecting human rights

There is a belief that sovereign states are an enemy of human rights, and that the construction of a world community which rises above the sovereign states system is necessary to emancipate humankind. An examination of historical and legal evidence suggests, to the contrary, that human rights protection depends heavily upon the capability of sovereign states and the responsibility of their governments. Human rights or natural rights, to use the older term, were conceived by people who understood the state as an organization for safeguarding civil society. They perceived worlds beyond the reach of effective and accountable state jurisdiction as less secure and more callous. Those outer worlds were more likely to be uncivil than civil. Where human rights are protected the people involved are likely to be living inside sovereign states that are worthy of the name. Nowadays such states typically are democracies which observe Thomas Hobbes's dictum: 'the safety of the people is the supreme law'. They go beyond Hobbes by including 'the freedom and dignity of all people' in the humanitarian mandate of statecraft.

Sovereign states are expected to be havens or sanctuaries where people can live out their lives free from threats and acts of plunder, predation, and brutalization. A fundamental responsibility of statesmen and stateswomen is to uphold the safety, freedom, and dignity of people, certainly their own people but increasingly nowadays other people too. There can be no guarantees, of course, because sovereign states are human organizations and are therefore subject to human frailties and failings. Some states are chaotic and barely states at all: failed states (Rotberg 2002). Some states are metaphorical prison houses and the population are inmates: totalitarian states. When states deteriorate and fall apart or governments become arbitrary and abusive, the human rights of the affected population are put at risk. And when that does happen, other states and the international organizations of states, such as the United Nations or the North Atlantic Treaty Organization, often express their concern. They may even be called upon to correct the situation, for example by foreign intervention (Wheeler 2000). A paradox of the sovereign state is that it can bring about both human flourishing and human suffering. But human rights violations caused by chaotic states or abusive states cannot be addressed or corrected by abandoning the state.

In theory human rights and state sovereignty are distinct and separate: we possess those rights in virtue of our humanity and regardless of our citizenship. In practice, however, they are connected: human rights are of practical significance, and consequence, because they have been recognized by positive law, both domestic law and international law. Insofar as human rights are enforced, that too is a primary responsibility of sovereign states and the international organizations established by such states. There are no other guardians of human rights whose historical significance or practical consequence even begins to compare with sovereign states. No other organizations, either public or private, possess the authority and the power that is necessary to perform that service for humanity.

Humanity discourse

My focus is the *practice* of human rights, as indicated by ordinary English usage and by positive law, national and international. I shall confine my discussion to the liberal conception of human rights as justifiable claims that belong to individual human beings *as such*: their natural or inherent rights. An empirical way to approach humanity discourse is via the *Oxford English Dictionary Online* (*OED*), which is our most important source of information on English vocabulary, both historical and contemporary. The *OED* traces and records the usage of words, in this case 'rights', 'human', 'humanity', and related expressions.

Any discussion of human rights should first come to terms with what it means to speak of 'rights'. According to the *OED*, 'rights' are 'what one may properly claim; one's due'. That recalls Immanuel Kant's notion of a 'right' as 'an assurance that each individual receives . . . what is his due' (Reiss 1991: 135). To possess a 'right' is to have a 'justifiable title or claim to something', such as an individual's claim to safety, freedom, and dignity, which are vital human rights. The same basic idea, focused on the political community instead of the individual person, is involved in a sovereign state's claim to independence, self-defence, and non-intervention.

What do English speakers mean when they use the expressions 'human', 'humanity', and 'human rights'? The *OED* begins with three fundamental distinctions in that regard. A 'human' is a creature 'distinguished from animals by superior mental development, power of articulate speech, and upright posture'. Human beings are also 'distinguished from God or superhuman beings'. Humans are mortal, not immortal. Their lives can be endangered or even taken from them by aggressive, cruel, or predatory people: they can be threatened, tortured, or killed. (Their lives can also be taken by non-human creatures and by acts of nature – but that is another story.) Vulnerability and exposure to harm is an inherent characteristic of human existence that explains why the most basic of all human rights are the rights to be safe and out of danger as far as that is possible in practice. 'Activities, relationships, etc. which are observable in mankind' should also be distinguished from 'machinery or the mechanical element'. Humans are not means or tools to be used or exploited for instrumental purposes. The freedom and dignity of people must be recognized and respected and cannot be lightly or contemptuously or cynically dismissed.

A very important human right is the right not to be reduced to slavery or serfdom or some other instrumental status or sub-human existence ('Supplementary Convention on the Abolition of Slavery, the Slave Trade, and Institutions and Practices Similar to Slavery'). Medieval serfdom was gradually abolished by the sovereign states of modern Europe. Slavery and especially slave transporting and slave trading of non-Europeans and particularly Africans was for long a lawful practice, but that too was abolished by the efforts of some sovereign states and most notably Britain, in response to parliamentary pressure and public opinion. The Slavery Abolition Act (1833) liberated all slaves in the British Empire. The emancipation of slaves in the United States is another major chapter in the story. The thirteenth Amendment of the Constitution (1865) abolished slavery. Household slavery, clandestine enslavement, and slave trafficking still exist in some places. What also exist are various forms of servitude that mostly affect children, what the Anti-Slavery Society describes as 'virtual slavery'. But no state recognizes the legal right of one person to claim another person as his or her property (Anti-Slavery Society 2006).

That supremely important episode in the history of human rights registers a clear echo of Kant: 'But a man is not a thing, that is to say, something which can be used merely as [a] means, but must in all his actions be always considered as an end in himself' (Kant 2006: second section, 4). That is the principle of humanity. That principle has been incorporated into domestic law and international law by sovereign states and the states system. It does not exist and arguably it could not exist *in practice* outside that framework. That is because the emancipation of slaves, for example, required legal authority as well as military and police power, both of which are in the possession and control of sovereign states. Britain could abolish slavery within its empire because it was the sovereign authority. It could suppress the maritime traffic of slave traders between Africa and the Americas because the Royal Navy held sway over the Atlantic Ocean.

What is the 'character or quality of being human'? The answer is to be found in the ways humans are expected to relate to each other and to act toward each other. In English usage, according to the *OED*, members of 'humanity' are expected to engage in 'behaviour . . . as befits a human being'. Instances of that behaviour include 'civility, courtesy, politeness' or 'friendly acts' or 'obligingness'. That vocabulary illuminates what it is to be 'humane', which is a 'disposition to treat human beings . . . with consideration and compassion, and to relieve their distresses'. It is showing 'kindness' and displaying 'benevolence'.

There is another facet of humanity, the dark side, which is captured in the English expression 'man's inhumanity to man'. Words that disclose that negative quality include 'contempt', 'incivility', 'hostility', 'hurt', and 'hate'. Such words mark proclivities, actions, and relations that are 'inhumane' or 'inhuman', defined by the *OED* as 'not having the qualities proper or natural to a human being; especially . . . kindness or pity'. Instead, what we find are hostile inclinations and hurtful actions, such as those which are 'brutal, unfeeling, cruel . . . savage, barbarous'. 'Inhumanity' is 'want of human feeling and compassion; brutality, barbarous cruelty'. This darker side is captured by the expression 'human wrongs', which is just as important as the notion of 'human rights' for obtaining an accurate picture of what it means to be human, what it is to live one's life as a human being, and what is involved in a failure to do so (Booth 1995: 103–26).

Human rights, in the classical way of thinking, exist independently of whatever positive legal rights, either domestic or international, that individuals may or may not possess. The Roman Stoic philosopher Cicero put the point in its most memorable formulation: 'there will not be different laws at Rome or Athens, or different laws now and in the future, but one eternal and unchangeable law will be valid for all nations and for all times' (Cicero 1950: 3.22). Here is an early statement of natural law. In the same vein, the *OED* refers to the doctrine *humanitas et universitas* and quotes Thomas Paine (1985: 24) in *Rights of Man*: 'these natural, imprescriptible, and unalienable rights [of man]'. 'Imprescriptible' signifies that human acts, either of individuals or organizations, including state laws and policies, cannot repudiate or invalidate or erase 'natural rights'. The conditions and characteristics of 'humanity' are therefore understood to be universal and unchanging – whether individuals are male or female, African or European, young or old, Christian or Moslem, capitalist or socialist, educated or uneducated, and so forth. Human rights – according to the standard doctrine – are part of human nature *as such*. They are held, equally, by all human beings, without exception, and regardless of the circumstances, such as the time and the place in which they happen to live.

This brief review of English usage focuses our attention on the vulnerability of the human condition, and on human beings' justifiable claim to recognition and respect. An individual may be said to have a human right to protection, but that will not be of much practical value without a protector. If human rights were generally respected, such organized means would be unnecessary. Regrettably that has not been the case in the past, nor is it the case today. The practical problem of human rights is that they need to be recognized and safeguarded in some way. Merely by acknowledging that we ought to respect such rights, as a moral duty, is not sufficient to generate respect.

What is required is not only the support of other individuals and private organizations but also and even more so the recognition of human rights by authoritative and credible public organizations with powers of enforcement and the will to act accordingly. Here is where the sovereign state enters the equation. State involvement is crucial because, as Thomas Hobbes pointed out long ago, 'the laws of nature, in the state of nature, are silent' (1993: 165–6). An organized state authority with sufficient will and power is required to give natural law an authoritative voice that will be heard and heeded by most people. Thomas Paine agrees with Thomas Hobbes and claims that the sovereign state exists primarily for that purpose. He speaks of 'the end of all political associations' as 'the preservation of the natural and imprescriptible rights of man' (Paine 1985: 45).

That is the classical liberal theory of the state as a defender of human rights. Sovereign states are required to give voice and weight to such rights, if they are to be enjoyed in practice. They have done that by legally recognizing the human rights of their people as civil rights, and also by protecting the human rights of all people under international law. Sovereign states have been legalizing human rights under statute law and constitutional law at least since the English Bill of Rights (1689), the French Declaration of the Rights of Man (1789), and the American Bill of Rights (1791). They have been acknowledging their commitment to international human rights protection at least since the United Nations Charter (1945) and the Universal Declaration of Human Rights (1948).

Human rights, human wrongs, and sovereign states

A primary way – almost the exclusive way – that we judge human conditions around the world is by reference to the sovereign states in which people are obliged to live. We classify and label countries by criteria related to the flourishing and the suffering of their populations. When we look at human rights protection we direct our attention to the policies and activities of governments. The nations of the world are ranked according to their performance in that regard. Some countries are judged to be highly desirable places in which most people flourish. Other countries are judged to be highly undesirable in which they languish and suffer.

The civil conditions of human safety, freedom, and dignity are most likely to exist and to be enjoyed if they are endorsed and enforced by sovereign states that are worthy of the name. Where else can people live and build their individual and collective lives with reasonable assurance of being protected and having their freedom and dignity respected, if never a complete guarantee, except in countries whose governments acknowledge and carry out their responsibilities in that regard? No other organizations developed since the start of the modern era have had anything like the same significance in performing those vital humanitarian services. Those long-standing political arrangements acknowledge human vulnerability, as described earlier, and attempt to compensate for it by their constitutions and laws, institutions and organizations, regulations and policies. Civil rights, the rights of citizenship underwritten by sovereign states, have been and remain the most assured rights that people can possess. Here, then, is a constructed political and legal order, which attempts to overcome and has had considerable success in overcoming the exposure and vulnerability of the natural or pre-civil condition of human beings. Here is where human rights are most assured of protection.

People are dependent on the sovereign state for providing their security, defending their freedom, and upholding their dignity; and to carry out its responsibilities in that regard, the sovereign has to be equipped with sufficient authority and power. It must have the 'sword of war' and the 'sword of justice' at its exclusive disposal. But those swords are double-edged. Sovereigns can fail in their responsibilities to their citizens or subjects. The laws can oppress the people. A fundamental and recurrent paradox of sovereign states is that they contain within themselves the potential for bringing about *both* human flourishing and human suffering. The sovereign state is a human organization, and as such it cannot be expected to escape from human frailties and failings. If anything, it deepens the dilemma by acquiring daunting power, particularly military power, which is placed in the hands of the people who govern.

When governments deal with people arbitrarily, contemptuously, harshly, or cruelly, the state itself becomes a major source of danger, to its own people first but to other states and their people as well. We need look no farther than the history of the twentieth century to find abundant evidence for that proposition. That recent period witnessed the extremes of human relations in a world of sovereign states: the depths of iniquity and injustice and the heights of magnanimity and sacrifice. Both extremes were displayed, time and again, during the same world-shaking episode: the Second World War. The Nazi conquest and occupation of most of Europe (1939–45) penetrated the underworld depths of human depravity and cruelty via policies of arbitrary arrest and imprisonment, torture and killing, slave labour camps, and, worst of all, genocide. The resistance to the occupation and the liberation of Europe demonstrated, in some of its finest moments, the heights to which human generosity can sometimes rise.

In the decades that followed that most destructive of all wars, the states of Western Europe turned around surprisingly quickly and by the 1960s most of their citizens were flourishing to a greater extent than they had prior to that war. A significant part of that achievement can be attributed to the post-war diplomatic, military, and economic policy of the United States. Washington undertook to uphold the security of post-war Western Europe against an expansive Soviet Union that occupied Eastern Europe following the defeat of Nazi Germany in that area by the Red Army in 1945. The heart of that security arrangement was the North Atlantic Treaty Organization (NATO), founded in 1949. The United States also resuscitated European societies, including extensively damaged industries and often destroyed infrastructure, by launching and funding the Marshall Plan for European political and economic recovery (1947), which aimed not only at the recovery of the market economy but also at the restoration of the rule of law and the institution of democracy.

The responsibility for that remarkable post-war achievement can also be claimed by Western Europe's re-established or reconstituted sovereign states. In the decades following the war they succeeded in establishing standards of living for their citizens which today are among the highest anywhere, if they are not indeed the highest. That is an achievement of those states both individually via their domestic laws and policies, and collectively via post-war international organizations they established for that purpose. Those states individually recognize and respect the civil rights of their citizens without exception. Collectively they established the most substantial international human rights organization in the world: the European Court of Human Rights located in Strasbourg which is part of the Council of Europe (1949). They also founded the European Union (1957), the most significant international organization of its kind, which is concerned not only with economic integration and prosperity but also with democracy and human rights.

Even granting the regrettable truth of the persistent if not permanent humanitarian problem posed by the temptation, corruption, and abuse of state power, there is no proven alternative to state sovereignty as a political and legal arrangement for providing the best assurance of human safety, freedom, and dignity – at least there is none of which I am aware. Human beings have flourished to the greatest extent yet known to history when they live under the authority of reliable and responsible sovereign states. Nowadays that is most obviously the case in those countries that we refer to as democracies. The best places to live in the contemporary world as judged by humanitarian standards – the safest, the freest, the most decent, and the most prosperous – are the countries of Western Europe, North America, Japan, Australia, New Zealand, and other such places.

Human rights under international law

The greater part of international law – what used to be called the law of nations – is concerned first and foremost with sovereign states: it has been defined as 'the body of rules and principles of action which are binding upon . . . states in relations with one another' (Brierly 1936: 1). Sovereign states are the paramount legal subjects – although not the exclusive legal subjects – of international relations. By their mutual recognition and intercourse (diplomacy), their contractual agreements and arrangements (treaties), and their common observances and practices (customary international law) over the past three or four centuries they have collaborated to construct a law unto themselves. There is no cosmopolitan 'law of humanity' that stands above the positive international law of sovereign states. Today, however, international law is also a law for humanity: individual people are international legal subjects, which they were not to any significant extent prior to the establishment of the international human rights regime starting in the mid-twentieth century.

International law conceives of state sovereignty in terms of 'the ownership of rights' (Brownlie 1979: 111–12). Among the most important of such rights are: the right of territorial jurisdiction and non-intervention (which excludes the authority and the activities of foreign powers from one's territory without one's consent), rights of embassy and diplomatic immunity, rights of war (which are a monopoly of sovereign states and the international organizations of such states), rights of commerce, the right over natural resources, the right of passage, fishing rights, and so on. International law involves such matters as legal personality and status, recognition of states and governments, the creation and transfer of sovereignty, privileges and immunities of states, the responsibilities of states, citizenship and nationality, the Most-Favoured-Nation rule, the law of the sea, judicial settlement of international disputes – among other matters in regard to which states have legitimate interests and concerns. This is only a small selection from a long list of international legal topics and issues. Sovereign states are without a doubt the most important rights holders under international law. They are no longer the only rights holders, for they now share that standing with human beings. But that change was made possible by sovereign states.

International human rights law is a law of sovereign states that is fundamentally concerned with the safety, freedom, and dignity of individual human beings and with the obligations of states in that regard. It is an important international response of sovereign states to the vulnerability of all people regardless of the country in which they happen to live. Human rights are recognized by international law and are promoted by international organizations, and that has been clearly evident since 1945. Previously they existed largely as a moral doctrine under the name of 'natural law'. But human rights have not been given pride of place in international law. That still belongs to the rights of sovereign states. In a leading textbook on international law, the rights of 'the individual' are not extensively discussed until chapter 24 (Brownlie 1979: 552–98). All previous chapters deal with the rights of states. When the individual does finally make an appearance, it is in relation to the international responsibility of states to protect human rights. The word 'protection' is a key to understanding human rights under international law. Sovereign states, individually and collectively, are the authorities and agencies with the legal responsibility of protecting human rights around the world.

Before we proceed any farther it is necessary to notice an important distinction between international human rights law and international humanitarian law. Both of these bodies of international law exist 'to protect the individual from arbitrary action and abuse' (ICRC 2006). The former is concerned with human vulnerability at all times and places. Nowadays human rights are recognized by the greater number of sovereign states and codified in various bodies of international law, both global and regional. The latter is concerned with curbing and restraining armed hostilities so as to limit individual human suffering, of both soldiers and civilians, in times and places of war (Roberts and Guelff 1989). Most of it is contained in the Hague Conventions (1899, 1907) and the Geneva Conventions and Protocols (1949). During times of war or situations of armed conflict international human rights law and international humanitarian law apply in a complementary and mutually reinforcing manner. In times of peace, however, only the former applies.

This chapter is mainly concerned with international human rights law. But it is important to emphasize that both these bodies of human-focused international law have been made by sovereign states and by no other law-making bodies. That they have constructed laws of war should come as no surprise, since sovereign states have long been and still remain the principal war-making agencies in human affairs. That they have legally recognized humanitarian concerns and human rights, both in war and in peace, is an indication of the extent to which they have become cognizant of and in some instances even bound by the principle of humanity. Today human rights are a significant international legal category. The twentieth-century society of sovereign states made that possible.

As indicated, the primary sphere for safeguarding the rights of individuals long has been and continues to be the domestic jurisdictions of capable and law-abiding sovereign states, where they are legally instituted as civil rights. Since 1945, however, there has been a secondary sphere where human rights have been protected up to a point, although more tenuously: namely that of international human rights law. That was a specific response of sovereign states to almost unbelievable acts of inhumanity that were carried out by aggressive and abusive totalitarian states during the Second World War, particularly the genocide policies of Nazi Germany. That may help explain why international human rights protection is more substantially evident in Europe than anywhere else. That should also be read in the context of the history of civil rights, which are the inherent rights of the individual recognized by domestic law. Western European states (together with the United States) have a lengthy history of legally acknowledging and protecting the rights of citizens, a tradition which in some countries goes back to the eighteenth century, even to the late seventeenth century in the case of the English Bill of Rights, which in part is entitled 'An Act Declaring the Rights and Liberties of the Subject'. International law has extended that traditional responsibility of states to include the protection of people in foreign countries. The principal authorities and agencies charged with the protection of individual rights – sovereign states – are still the same, however.

By far the most significant and successful body of international human rights law is the European Convention for the Protection of Human Rights and Fundamental Freedoms (1950), which is an international bill of rights for the population of member states of the Council of Europe (Brownlie 1979: 574). At the time of writing all the signatories, with the exception of Ireland and Norway, had incorporated the Convention into their own law. The European Court of Human Rights has the authority, under certain specified legal circumstances, to overturn decisions of High Courts or Supreme Courts of member states. Litigants who complain that their rights have been infringed by a state party to the Convention, and that they have not received justice in that state's judicial bodies, can bring their case to the Court. Signatory states can also bring their case. The Court may decide whether or not to adjudicate the case. The judgments of the Court are legally binding on member states. It is the only international human rights regime about which that can be said. The regime, including the authority of such judicial decisions, nevertheless rests entirely on the prior consent of those states that have joined the Council of Europe and subjected themselves to the decisions of the European Court of Human Rights. The regime is built on a foundation of sovereign states and could not have been built in any other way.

The international law of human rights should therefore be understood as a further legal barrier erected by sovereign states and intended to keep individuals safe and free from harm or abuse, regardless of where they happen to live. That means that states which refuse or fail to protect the rights of their own people must expect foreign governments or international organizations to be concerned. That also means that such governments and organizations must be prepared to protect human rights wherever they are threatened or violated, either at home or abroad. It must be so if human rights protection is a general international norm consistent with the universal vulnerability of human beings, which arguably it now is. But that is easier to contemplate in theory than to realize in practice. The next section expands on this point.

This leads to a comment on the place of non-governmental organizations (NGOs) in the international protection of human rights. They have an important humanitarian role, of course, but it is a secondary and auxiliary role to that of sovereign states. NGOs have influence, they can make their views known to states and to international organizations, they can give advice, they can call attention to humanitarian crises and issues. As legal consultants or technical experts, they can help draft international law on human rights issues (as well as other issues, such as environmental protection) if states or international organizations consult them. Private individuals and voluntary organizations played an instrumental role in drafting the Universal Declaration of Human Rights and other bodies of international human rights law. As relief agencies, NGOs can attempt to do whatever good they can wherever they manage to operate around the world. Wherever they do operate, however, they depend upon permission and protection from state authorities or international organizations.

What humanitarian NGOs cannot do is make the law, for they have no legal authority. Nor can they take upon themselves the responsibility of providing human rights enforcement by the exercise of military and police power. They are not military or police organizations. They have no legal right to bear arms. Although they can of course send their staff to various countries around the world, NGOs (like the rest of us) ultimately depend on sovereign governments for permission to enter countries and carry out humanitarian operations within them. They are not free to operate wherever and whenever they wish. They also depend upon national and international authorities for the protection of their staff in dangerous places. That was particularly obvious in Somalia in the early 1990s, when the Somali state collapsed and a dangerous situation of internal war waged by rival warlords came into existence. NGOs in Somalia were exposed to that danger. They made urgent appeals to the United Nations and to the United States and other countries to intervene to protect not only the Somali people but also their staffs who were caught in the crossfire. NGOs depend, like everyone else depends, on the sovereign state system for the recognition and protection of their human rights.

Humanitarian intervention

The international enlargement of sovereign state responsibility to protect individuals and their rights, regardless of their citizenship or place of residence, has created some thorny normative issues, the most controversial being that of humanitarian intervention involving the use of armed force. Some issues stem from the fact that states have many rights of their own, including most importantly the above-noted right of territorial jurisdiction and non-intervention, which cannot be ignored or swept aside but must be considered alongside human rights. Other issues derive from the fact that states have many responsibilities besides the responsibility to protect individual human rights around the world. Two of the most important are their responsibilities to defend their own people and to uphold international peace and security. Yet another controversy grows out of what is perhaps the most difficult – and tragic – fact of all: that human rights can be violated by sovereign states or by international organizations in the course of employing armed force for humanitarian purposes.

States are now expected, indeed they are charged under international human rights law, not only with the responsibility of protecting their citizens and foreign residents on their territories but with that of protecting the citizens or residents of foreign countries as well. They are not expected to sacrifice their own citizens to aid or rescue citizens and residents of foreign countries. But they are expected to be concerned and to take whatever action they can to defend the human rights of those foreigners when they are under threat or attack in a significant way. Those dual responsibilities are almost bound to involve normative predicaments and even dilemmas at some point. How much can independent governments demand of their citizens in their efforts to defend international human rights? As a practical matter I believe it is accurate to say they cannot demand too much – unless vital interests (such as national security) are also at stake. In that case, however, sovereign state rights and human rights are not in conflict. But how much is too much and how much is too little? There is no clear and consistent answer in international practice. The scope of territorial jurisdiction and the range of international humanitarian responsibility of states are controversial subjects.

However, it is possible to outline two noteworthy recent approaches to the issue of humanitarian intervention, by practitioners, which attempt to find a resolution to the controversy – or if not a resolution then at least a reasonable way of judging the issue. The starting point for each approach is the same: the responsibilities of sovereign states to protect people living outside their borders as well as those living inside. Both approaches reject the proposition that sovereign states today have an absolute right of non-intervention. From that common point of departure, however, they diverge.

The first and more progressive approach, 'the responsibility to protect' doctrine, is spelled out in the widely disseminated *Report of the International Commission on Intervention and State Sovereignty* (Evans and Sahnoun: 2001). It argues that there can be consistency and coordination between state sovereignty and human rights, even as regards the difficult and controversial question of humanitarian intervention. The doctrine is recognizably Kantian in that regard. The second and more pragmatic approach has no name but it could be labelled 'the balance of state responsibilities and human rights' doctrine. Although it is not conveniently contained in any one basic document, it can be detected in certain commentaries on humanitarian intervention, particularly those contained in *Humanitarian Intervention: Legal and Political Aspects* (DUPI 1999). It argues that state sovereignty and human rights can be expected to be in conflict and even to collide from time to time, and that is nowhere more evident than in cases of humanitarian intervention. The problem is to find an acceptable or at least a tolerable balance between state sovereignty and human rights. The doctrine is recognizably Aristotelian in that regard. The two doctrines can only be discussed in brief.

The first approach notes that state sovereignty involves heavy responsibilities, and that the primary responsibility of sovereign states is to protect people within their own borders. But that is not the end of their responsibility to protect, which extends across international borders and involves safeguarding people under threat or attack in whatever country they happen to live. Vulnerability and insecurity is a universal predicament of human beings, which necessitates a general responsibility to protect, especially now that the means of protection exists, namely rapidly deployable and highly mobile military force in the possession of some member states of international society. Where a foreign population is suffering serious harm – as a result of internal war, insurgency, repression, or state failure – and the local state is unable or unwilling to deal with it, the sovereign right of territorial jurisdiction and non-intervention 'must yield to the international responsibility to protect'. The objective of such armed intervention should always be the protection of a population, never the overthrow of a government or regime – or the advancement of the national interest of an intervening state.

The legal foundations of the responsibility to protect are obligations inherent in state sovereignty, which is the source of international law. They are embodied in the responsibility of the UN Security Council to uphold and defend international peace and security. Human security – personal safety of individuals wherever they happen to be located – is seen to be part of international peace and security (Jackson 2000a: 210–15). It is no longer confined to domestic jurisdiction, which is the traditional argument. Those obligations are enshrined in declarations, conventions, covenants, and treaties of international human rights law and international humanitarian law. They are evident in the humanitarian activities of states, regional organizations, and the United Nations.

The responsibility to protect is a doctrine for justifying humanitarian intervention by making the sovereign right of non-intervention conditional on the state's responsibility to protect its population. If states refuse or fail to exercise that responsibility, they make themselves subject to the possibility of lawful international intervention. The doctrine calls for international deployment of military forces to protect people exposed to credible and grave danger, wherever they may be living. Military intervention for humanitarian protection is recognized as 'an exceptional and extraordinary measure'. To be necessary and obligatory, there must be 'serious and irreparable harm occurring to human beings' or 'imminently likely to occur'. Such acts or threats would include: actual or threatened large scale loss of life, with or without genocidal intent, as a result of deliberate government action, or neglect, or inability to act, or a 'failed state situation', or 'large scale "ethnic cleansing"', whether carried out by killing, by forced expulsion, or by acts of terror or rape'.

According to the responsibility to protect doctrine, there is 'no better or more appropriate body' than the UN Security Council 'to authorize military intervention for human protection purposes'. The doctrine seeks to provide a more relevant moral and legal rationale, than exists within the current UN framework, for authorizing military action for international humanitarian protection. 'The task is not to find alternatives to the Security Council as a source of authority, but to make the Security Council work better than it has.' That requires full cooperation of the permanent members of the Security Council, who 'should agree not to apply their veto power, in matters where their vital state interests are not involved, [and not] to obstruct the passage of resolutions authorizing military intervention for human protection purposes for which there is otherwise majority support.'

Here the Security Council is being assigned the responsibility to safeguard individual human beings around the world. That steps beyond its traditional responsibility to uphold international peace and security, defined as peace and security *between* countries. In addition the Council is now expected to uphold peace and security *within* countries. The international responsibility to protect doctrine assumes that Security Council members would be willing, and that at least some of them would be able to exercise the added burden of safeguarding human security in foreign countries. There is an empirical basis for that assumption. Since the end of the Cold War the Council has been revising the 1945 UN Charter norm for judging a 'threat' to 'international peace and security' (Art. 39). In a series of Resolutions that norm has been expanded, in effect, to include humanitarian crises as well as terrorism and weapons of mass destruction as threats (United Nations Report of the High-level Panel on Threats, Challenges and Change 2004). A radical and arguably unrealistic element of this argument is its proposal to override the veto of the five permanent members and base Security Council decisions regarding humanitarian intervention on majority votes. That would be a fundamental change of the original 1945 constitution of the Security Council as laid down in chapter VII of the UN Charter.

The second and more pragmatic approach, the balance of state responsibilities and human rights doctrine, argues that sovereign states and international organizations have a responsibility to protect human beings wherever that is possible and permissible. At the back of that approach – although not explicitly acknowledged – is what Isaiah Berlin has termed a 'collision of values' (Berlin 1992: 13). The system or society of sovereign states is seen to encompass an assortment of legitimate interests and concerns, some compatible, some not compatible. All sovereign states, by their very nature, have multiple goals to pursue and diverse interests to defend. Their responsibility to protect people in foreign countries necessarily must be balanced against other important responsibilities they have. The most important are their responsibilities to protect their citizens and not to put at risk unnecessarily the lives of their soldiers. Here necessity is conventionally understood as geared, first and foremost, to the security and survival of one's own state and its people. International activity to protect people must be taken in that pluralistic and sometimes contradictory context.

The second approach pays attention to the fact that individual human rights and sovereign state rights may come into conflict and may even collide – which could produce difficult normative dilemmas. It also notes that sovereign states have important and legitimate interests which, on occasion, may require neglect and perhaps even sacrifice of human rights. Such occasions are most evident during times of threatened or actual war, when situations arise that may call for, may even demand military actions that put non-combatants in harm's way. Under certain circumstances it may be unavoidable or even necessary to sacrifice the human rights of some people to protect the human rights of other people.

According to this second doctrine, there are no absolute values or trump norms in world affairs, and that includes human rights as well as state sovereignty. Humanitarian intervention tragically may involve human rights violations. In the air war over Kosovo (1999), NATO bombing killed non-combatants (Jackson 2000b). That (presumably) was a calculated risk of a military policy that required NATO pilots to drop their bombs from a sufficiently high altitude to protect them from anti-aircraft artillery and missiles. That increased the likelihood of 'collateral damage' and the maiming or killing of civilians in proximity to target areas. However, there was more to the normative dilemma than that. The humanitarian norm of non-combatant immunity (which in this episode affected mostly Serbian civilians in the vicinity of NATO bombardment targets) was evidently sacrificed out of higher regard, not only for the lives of the pilots but also for the humanitarian military objective they were trying to reach. They were trying to save Kosovar Albanians from ongoing ethnic cleansing by armed Serbian authorities and militias operating in Kosovo, an integral territory of Serbia. They were aiming to make it possible for NATO ground forces to occupy Kosovo and correct the injustice of ethnic cleansing by creating conditions of peace, order, and law which would allow the refugees to return to their villages and homes. The human rights of some people were put at risk to safeguard the human rights of other people.

Another humanitarian dilemma was evident, on a much larger scale, in the military invasion, occupation, and attempted pacification of Iraq by armed forces of the United States and Britain. That episode resulted in far greater civilian casualties, a number running into many thousands and estimated by some to be a hundred thousand or more. This time the beneficiaries and the victims of armed intervention were from among the same people, the Iraqis. And the choice that eventually presented itself, although unclear at first, was not a choice between the dictatorship of Saddam Hussein and the blessings of regime change and a newly founded democracy made possible by foreign military intervention. Rather, the choice was between human wrongs: the wrongs of dictatorship versus the wrongs of anarchy and chaos inadvertently unleashed by the intervention. These episodes bring to light the difficulties, perplexities, and very mixed blessings involved in employing armed force to protect the human rights of people in other countries.

A discernible difficulty with this argument is its silence on how tolerable balances can be struck between state sovereignty and human rights, or between some people's human rights and other people's human rights, in real situations where they come into conflict. That would be the critique of rationalist moral utilitarianism or cost/benefit approaches to foreign policy. A fundamental implication of this second doctrine, however, is that such dilemmas are inescapable, and that the best that one can do is to face them with human compassion and an acute sense of responsibility.

My purpose in briefly outlining these two doctrines of humanitarian intervention is not to invite a choice between them and much less is it to draw a conclusion that one is superior to the other. Nor is my purpose to examine any criteria which might be used to assess the weight that should be given, respectively, to state sovereignty and to human rights, or to one person's human rights and another person's human rights, when they are in conflict. Those exercises are beyond the scope of this study. My purpose is to emphasize that the protection of human rights in world affairs is heavily dependent on the foreign policies and international activities of sovereign states. Whichever of these doctrines we might ourselves settle on, they both have the merit of taking the existing framework of state sovereignty as a point of departure in seeking to justify the use of armed force to protect human rights around the world. There is no realistic alternative.

6
Sovereignty and Globalization

9/11 and the state

On September 11 2001, Americans were shocked into a Hobbesian awareness of what sovereign states basically are for. Their ramparts – the highest and strongest in the world – had been dramatically breached, not by another great power but by a tiny band of terrorists. On that transfixing occasion Americans did not revert to the state of nature and head for the hills. They did not call upon the International Committee of the Red Cross or Amnesty International or any other humanitarian or human rights organization. Living in the citadel of capitalism they did not turn to Wall Street or George Soros. They turned to Washington and George W. Bush. They turned to the president, the congress, the military, the police, the diplomats, the spies, and the other government authorities and agencies available to them. Their government turned to friends and allies abroad, many of whom also were targets of terrorism, for collaboration and assistance in a common effort to stamp it out. In the events that followed September 11 the fundamental role of the sovereign state as protector and safe haven was clear to everyone.

In the sort of world in which we live, global and inter-connected, states that face a security crisis may and very likely they will count on the assistance of their allies and the cooperation of other states in attempting to deal with it. That was evident in the swift decision of the North Atlantic Treaty Organization in response to the attack on New York and Washington. On September 12 NATO invoked, for the first time in its fifty-two-year history, Article 5 of its treaty: that an attack against any member of the alliance shall be considered an attack against all of them. The irony that weaker NATO members were coming to the aid of the United States, rather than the reverse, was not lost upon observers ('Terrorist Attacks Redefine Common Wisdom about Transatlantic Security'). Washington also turned to Pakistan, Russia, Egypt, Khazakstan, Kuwait, India, Indonesia, and other countries for assistance and cooperation in the fight against terrorism. The international nature of the episode was evident, too, in a warning that foreign governments that sponsor terrorism or serve as shelters for terrorists or resign themselves to their presence on their territory – instead of suppressing them – could face foreign intervention ('Terrorism: Questions and Answers').

It would be difficult to make sense of terrorism and the response to the terrorist attacks on Nairobi, Moscow, New York and Washington, Bali, Madrid, Ankara, London, Amman, Mumbai, and other places without presupposing the fundamental security responsibilities of sovereign states and the states system. That is so even though a 'war' on international terrorism poses awkward problems for sovereign states, which are adapted for making war with each other and against one another, not against non-state actors. But it is easy to discern the targets of international terrorism: the governments and citizens of sovereign states. In their very designs and actions terrorists are postulating the significance and importance of such states. A practical legal problem in dealing with terrorism is deciding whether terrorists are warriors – as they claim to be – or criminals. Whatever the decision may be, it can be taken entirely from within the framework of state sovereignty, which is an institution arranged to deal with both war and criminality (United States Patriot Act of Congress).

A basic assumption and expectation of state sovereignty is security of the nation and its citizens. The standard in that regard is set by the relatively successful and substantial states of Europe and North America as well as Japan, Australia, New Zealand, among others. That assumption is made in spite of the fact that in some cases it does not hold up very well or at all. Certain governments, often located on the periphery of the states system, cannot or will not provide security throughout their territory. There are quasi-states propped up by the international system, states in a condition of internal war, failed states that to all intents and purposes have ceased to exist, and various other situations where security across the country patently cannot be supposed (Jackson 1990). Every state is in some respects a failure, of course, insofar as it does not routinely enforce the law in every corner of its jurisdiction with total effectiveness. A completely successful state, an entirely secure person or population, is a concept, not a reality. In some American cities after dark there are 'no go' areas beyond the control of civil authority that are dangerous to enter and which recollect Hobbes's 'state of nature' (Hobbes 1946: ch. 13). Where domestic security is not made available by the state it is usually understood to be an urgent problem that ought to be corrected. Security is a presupposition of sovereign statehood. Insecurity is a sign of state weakness, lack of will, loss of control, collapse, failure. We notice that and decry it as a regrettable and perhaps intolerable departure from what is expected.

Is it reasonable to suppose that some other arrangement of military and police power could take the place of the sovereign state and the states system in providing security? Globalization and non-state actors are not an alternative. The provision of security is beyond the capability of non-state actors who depend on the state for their security like everybody else. Terrorists may appear to be an exception, but they must operate from *terra firma* somewhere, and they usually try to find safe havens within states that support them or tolerate them or lack the will or capacity to suppress them. The globalization argument usually takes security as a given, and goes on from there. In doing so it is assuming the fundamental role and responsibility of the state, and the states system. Even recognizing that every state is a failure in some respects, I find it difficult to imagine a realistic and practical alternative. Better the devil we know. I say that while recognizing the main hazard of the state, every state including democracies, which is the abuse of its power by those in charge of it (Krieger 1967: 419). If Leviathan does not perform as required there usually is hell to pay. Even if we could come up with an alternative, perhaps some arrangement of global governance, it too would entail instrumental power and the risk of its abuse no matter how it is organized or who is involved with it.

Sovereign states, at their most fundamental, must be equipped with 'the sword of war' or 'the right to arm', and 'the sword of justice' or 'the right to punish', as Hobbes puts it (Hobbes 1993: 176–7). He captured this responsibility in the following words: 'Now, all the duties of rulers are contained in this one sentence, the safety of the people is the supreme law' (Hobbes 1993: 258). That proposition has not changed since the time of Hobbes, in spite of remarkable changes to states and societies in other respects. Hobbes is the political philosopher *par excellence* of the state as protector: the philosopher of security, safety, order, peace. 'The state is the unit of accountability in world affairs' (Schultz 2002). That remark of a former United States Secretary of State is as good an answer as any I have been able to come up with in response to the question of why we continue to rely on sovereign states and the states system. They are accountable and answerable for our security and other vital conditions and services that we cannot provide for ourselves. Arguably they are the only ones who could be. That may seem obvious, but attempting to explain the obvious, rather than merely taking it for granted, is a scholarly exercise worth undertaking.

The globalization thesis

Is the sovereign states system declining or on the verge of doing so? Are the foundations of that system – state sovereignty – weakening, eroding, even disintegrating and disappearing? Are we experiencing a great transformation in that regard (Burgi and Golub 2000)? Or is only the furniture and some of the architecture undergoing change? Is state sovereignty evolving, yet again, in response to scientific, technological, economic, and social changes – as it has done throughout the post-medieval era of its existence? I raise these questions because there are academics of different disciplines, experts of various kinds, journalists, businessmen, and at least some politicians who think we are experiencing a transformation of the sovereign states system into something different – even if it is unclear what that post-sovereign political world can be expected to look like in detail (Cooper 2002, Del Rosso 1995, Held 1995).

Nowadays it is often said that state sovereignty is in decline. International trade and commerce, multinational business, electronic telecommunications (telephones, satellites, the internet), transoceanic shipping and transcontinental transport, transnational organization, global travel and tourism, space exploration, increasing awareness of the world as a whole – all that and much else is said to be creating a global marketplace and cosmopolitan society that is bypassing and perhaps even displacing the sovereign state and states system. It is also pointed out that transnational criminality and international terrorism is persisting, even flourishing, in spite of efforts by states and the states system to stamp them out. In short, a new world beyond state jurisdiction and regulation is emerging that ever increasing numbers of people are involved with. State parochialism is giving way, rapidly or incrementally, to transnationalism and cosmopolitanism. Some scholars are foreseeing and even anticipating the emergence, in the not-too-distant future, of a democratic world authority resting on a supranational citizenship of some sort (Fukuyama 1991, Held 2004).

Today it is said that the state cannot manage international trade and commerce as it used to. Global markets set in motion tsunami waves of electronic money that encircle the earth beyond the purview and control of national governments. Multinational firms establish integrated trans-border production facilities and operations that escape from state regulation and taxation. Businesses in developed countries are 'outsourcing' their operations to developing countries. American and British publishers arrange for the editing and printing of their books in countries, such as India, where production costs, especially the cost of labour, are low. Labour markets are becoming global. In this scenario, capital moves without much hesitation to the most cost-effective available supply of labour. In another scenario, labour migrates to higher wages, which may be on the other side of an international border or across an ocean. It is said that the state cannot police – at least not as effectively as it once could – its territorial borders. Hosts of determined or desperate people find ways to enter countries illegally in search of employment. In recent years, for example, millions of Latin Americans have slipped into the United States, across its border with Mexico. A similar invasion has entered the European Union, across its southern and eastern frontiers.

There are some who argue that we are also witnessing the emergence of a 'global civil society' composed of organizations and activities – private, non-profit and voluntary – which occupy the 'social space' between the states system and the global marketplace (Salamon, Sokolowski, and List 2003). They point to human rights organizations, religious congregations, environmental groups, university-sponsored activities, voluntary groups of dedicated experts, including doctors and nurses who set up and run hospitals and clinics, teachers who organize and staff non-government schools, and engineers and technicians who design, build, or maintain local infrastructure. The number and variety of such organizations and activities have multiplied and spread in recent decades.

Some portray this as a 'global associational revolution', a 'massive upsurge of organized, private voluntary activity in virtually every region of the world' (Salamon, Sokdowski, and List 2003). These organizations and activities provide or foster basic goods and local services that governments and markets often fail or refuse to make available: clean water, local sanitation, elementary education, small-scale loans, simple technology, personal health care, public health awareness, social and even political consciousness, etc. They are said to be 'carving out' a distinctive 'space' for themselves, which is not confined by international boundaries or subjected to state regulations. They are seen to produce 'social capital': transnational bonds of trust and reciprocity that foster progressive change and development, including democracy, in their spheres of operation. According to this argument, that is because the sovereign state and states system is failing to respond to the basic needs of millions of people in the less developed world. Global capitalism sees no profit in responding. Transnational voluntarism is filling the void.

There is a parallel negative argument, not always recognized as such, which addresses the existence of a transnational uncivil society. The reference is to a shadowy underworld of actors that operate beyond the reach, without regard, even with contempt for national and international law. Organized bands of transnational criminals pose a challenge to law enforcement. Huge quantities of contraband goods find their way into countries. The most pervasive and entrenched transborder traffic is illicit drugs produced and distributed by criminal cartels, some of whom control significant territories within states, the Colombia drug barons being the most notorious example (United Nations Convention against Transnational Organized Crime). Pirates prey upon merchant vessels and cruise ships, presenting a threat to shipping and a challenge to maritime states. The end of Western imperialism reduced naval oversight of sea lanes in former colonial regions where piracy is once again flourishing, namely off the coasts of Africa, in the Caribbean, and along the waterways of South-East Asia (International Maritime Bureau). International terrorist groups threaten and carry out armed attacks against civilians in various countries. Insofar as terrorist groups must locate on the territory of specific countries (whether secretly or openly) to organize and prepare for their violent activities, they erode international confidence in the will or ability of the governments of those countries to police their own jurisdictions.

Such episodes are taken to indicate or at least to strongly hint at the emergence of a post-modern and post-sovereign world – a global economy, a transnational civil society, a transnational underworld – that escapes from the authority and the regulation we associate with the sovereign state, and the states system. No informed person could fail to recognize the important facts to which the globalization thesis draws our attention. The issue I wish to address concerns their interpretation. What I shall disagree with are a few key assumptions and inferences of the globalization thesis as it applies to the sovereign state and the states system. I shall argue that it is more reasonable to suppose and expect that the sovereign states system will adapt to globalization just as it adapted to previous transformations of science, technology, economy, and society. The main basis for my critique is historical.

Globalization is not unprecedented. Some features of global civil society and transnational underworld reach well into the past: world trade and traffic, religious missions, terrorism, criminality, and piracy. A flourishing worldwide economy, built on free trade and freedom of the seas, existed from the mid-nineteenth century – when the British Corn Laws and Navigation Acts were abolished – until the disruptions of the First World War and the protectionism of the Great Depression.[1] An earlier global seaborne economy, centred on Dutch and English mercantilism, flourished in the seventeenth century. The Dutch East India Company had 'factories' in what is today Russia, South-East Asia, the Caribbean, North and South America, and South Africa. Its vessels plied the waterways of the world. Much the same could be said of the British East India Company and other such chartered companies. As early as the sixteenth century Spanish and Portuguese explorers, soldiers, and traders were already exploiting the resources and riches of the Indies, West and East, and transporting them to Europe. The high technological basis of contemporary globalization makes possible a much faster moving and far more integrated world economy than those which existed previously. That is unprecedented. But it does not cancel the foregoing historical facts. Men and women along with their goods and chattels have been moving to and fro across the world for centuries.

As indicated, the globalization thesis contains an argument about the spread of private voluntary organizations and activities in less developed parts of the world, which provide urgently needed 'social capital' at the local level. Such activities are probably greater today than ever, but they are anything but new. Private Western charities were active in Asia, Africa, Latin America, the Caribbean, and the Pacific in the nineteenth century, and before that time in some places. Protestant missionary societies and certain monastic orders of the Catholic Church, the Jesuits and Dominicans for example, were active in the Americas from the sixteenth century, in Asia from the seventeenth and eighteenth centuries, and in Africa from the nineteenth century. Christian missionaries not only attempted to make converts but they provided basic services and amenities to the people they ministered. Most (but not all) of that human-focused activity – manifesting the spirit of *caritas* – existed under the aegis of Western imperial states (Cairns 1965).

As we might expect, the transnational underworld which operates by attacking, avoiding, or evading the state and market order is also deeply historical. The word 'terrorism' was coined during the French Revolution, and entered most European languages shortly afterwards. From the beginning terrorism targeted states as well as their subjects and citizens. Initially, it referred to violence by a revolutionary government which was determined to impose its ideology by eliminating political opposition – the infamous French Terror (1793–4) (*Oxford English Dictionary Online*). Later it came to signify assassination of political leaders, perhaps the most infamous case being the murder of Austrian Archduke Ferdinand by a Bosnian Serb student in Sarajevo in 1914. Criminals have been carrying on their activities across borders ever since territorial jurisdictions were created. Drug trafficking – legal and illegal – has a long history: opium from China, Turkey, India, and other such places was supplied to Western 'opium eaters' in the nineteenth century if not before. Piracy has a longer history: the laws against piracy are as old as international law itself – which dates to the late sixteenth and early seventeenth centuries (Rubin 1998, Johnson 1957).[2] These actors and activities, it should be noted, can only be understood as 'uncivil' or 'lawless' by reference to civil society and the rule of law.

From the start of the modern era, states and their agents – often chartered companies, such as the Dutch East India Company, founded in 1602, or the British East India Company, founded two years earlier – have been projecting their commercial and military power around the world, the effect of which has been to connect different parts of the world to an extent that never happened previously. Western imperialism – transoceanic and transcontinental imperial states – made most of that possible: by providing international order, by creating a world economy, by extending international law to the non-Western world, by territorial conquest, by entering into treaty and quasi-treaty relationships with indigenous authorities, by establishing protectorates and protected states, by setting up colonial governments, by making it possible for private charities and missionary societies to operate, and finally at the sunset of the era of Western empire by transferring sovereignty to former colonies. In short, the sovereign states system and globalization emerged and evolved together (Armstrong 1998).

The sovereign states system

Over the past three or four centuries ever more people have found themselves living in a world organized territorially as a system of sovereign states, which is a specifically European innovation. That system was eventually established in every populated corner of the planet (Bull and Watson). The European way of government became a global system, and the only one known to history. The entire planet was enclosed by it and still is.

That is very different from the era of its origins, when there were separate, self- affirming, and other-disdaining systems of authority and power in different parts of the non-European world, each one of which was a world unto itself. Among the most important were the Ottoman Empire in the Middle East, North Africa, and south-eastern Europe, the Chinese Empire and Tokugawa Japan in East Asia, and the Mogul Empire in South Asia. That possibility of separate, mutually spurning systems was brought to an end by Western powers in the nineteenth century. There were also far weaker indigenous empires – the Aztec and Inca empires in North and South America, for example – as well as numerous and various settled or nomadic peoples scattered across Siberia, the Americas, South-East Asia, tropical Africa, and Oceania. Over a lengthy period, beginning in the Americas in the sixteenth and seventeenth centuries and ending in Africa in the nineteenth century, they were enclosed by the Western states system, in the form of imperial dependencies of one kind or another. The final stage of expansion, which occurred in the nineteenth and twentieth centuries, involved recognizing as sovereign those previously nonconforming empires which escaped Western colonization, and transferring sovereignty over colonial dependencies to anti-colonial nationalists.

An international historian underlines the fundamental importance of that worldwide transformation:

> The great political fact of global history in the last 500 years is the emergence of a world of states from a world of empires. That fact – more than the expansion of democracy, more than nationalism, more than the language of rights, more even than globalization – fundamentally defines the political universe we all inhabit. (Armitage 2005: 1)

That world of sovereign states has existed without interruption, although greatly expanded and changed in important ways, since its formation in Western Europe in the sixteenth and seventeenth centuries. It has never been broken and destroyed or allowed to expire from natural causes or to collapse into the pre-modern world condition of mutually uncomprehending, disparaging, and non-communicating civilizations. Nor has it been transformed into World Empire or Global Federation. It has accommodated many different kinds of sovereign state over that lengthy period: monarchies, republics, military regimes, theocracies, imperial states, unitary states, federal states, democracies, dictatorships, and others besides. The number of sovereign states has contracted and expanded during that time. But the system itself has remained in existence continuously, without interruption. There is every indication it will persist indefinitely.

The global existence of the sovereign states system, its pre-emption of every separate or rival system of territorial authority and power, its enclosure of the entire land surface of the earth, is often seen – when noticed at all – as a commonplace and mundane fact. Viewed in the light of history it can only be regarded as an astounding development that discloses several features of a telling kind which have a bearing on the globalization thesis. They can be summarized only in the most general terms.

During the modern centuries it gradually became clear to non-Western rulers that undisturbed and uninvolved political existence beyond the Western states system was unsustainable, that it was impossible to remain aloof or keep the Western states at bay. That growing awareness was dictated by Western conquest, economic exploitation, military intimidation and protection, unequal treaties and extra-territoriality, colonial annexation and administration, and other impositions and inequalities which may be summarized as Western imperialism. But the system evidently could not stop evolving at those points. That arguably is for the same reason that once individual human beings (rather than groups) are a focus of morality, their full humanity cannot be denied, as in the case of slavery, but must be recognized, as in the form of human rights. In a world defined and ordered by state sovereignty, the only legitimate terminus is sovereign statehood for everybody. Various kinds of dependency status – such as protectorates and protected states, international mandates and trust territories, internal self-government – and any other qualified form of state authority short of independence is illegitimate. The earlier inclination of non-Europeans to resist annexation or other kinds of control by European sovereign states and their agents was thus followed much later, and somewhat ironically, by their desire and demand for full membership in the sovereign state system, with all its rights and privileges, on a basis of political and legal equality with Western states.

State sovereignty became a highly prized possession everywhere on the planet. It remains so to this day. That is registered in a high birth rate of sovereign states over the past century. During the imperial era the number of sovereign states reached a low point owing to the vast extent of the British, the French, the Portuguese, the Dutch, and the other Western empires, each of which was composed of multiple non-European territories under one European sovereign. The revolt against imperialism and the subsequent deconstruction of those empires consequently multiplied the number of sovereign states. This first occurred in North and South America in the eighteenth and nineteenth centuries. Many new states emerged in Eastern Europe after the First World War, the outcome of three connected, momentous episodes: the military defeat and dismantling of the Austro-Hungarian, German, and Turkish empires, the Russian Revolution, and American President Woodrow Wilson's ideology of national self-determination, which he brought to the Paris Peace Conference in 1919 (Nicolson 1945). Many more new or reconstituted states were a consequence of decolonization in Asia, the

Middle East, Africa, the Caribbean, and the Pacific following the Second World War. Still others emerged out of the disbanding of the Soviet Union – successor to the old Russian Empire which occupied a huge swathe of the Euro-Asian landmass – and the disintegration of Yugoslavia after the Cold War.

The desire and quest for full membership in the sovereign state system did not end with the foregoing episodes. It spread to sub-national groups and leaders who were not content merely to be a minority in an existing sovereign state but wanted to be exclusively sovereign themselves – or wanted to be part of the majority of a different sovereign state, usually a kindred state nearby. Thus partition, separatism, secession, and irredentism are also a feature of the system, and another indication of the premium placed on the possession of state sovereignty. That was matched, and usually exceeded, by the jealous and tenacious desire of existing sovereign states to keep intact their entire territory. Sometimes these conflicts led to war, the most consequential being the American Civil War (1861–5). Some sovereign states resulted from partition or secession: Ireland from the United Kingdom, India and Pakistan from British India, Jordan, Israel and (presumably) the Palestinian Authority from the British administered Palestine Mandate, Singapore from Malaysia, (West) Pakistan and Bangladesh (East Pakistan) from Pakistan, Eritrea from Ethiopia, the Czech Republic and Slovakia from Czechoslovakia. Secessionist campaigns for political independence continue to be carried on by Basque terrorists, Corsican patriots, Scottish nationalists, Québécois 'sovereigntists', Chechen separatists, various regional terrorists seeking independence from the Philippines, among other instances. Notwithstanding these campaigns, as indicated in chapter 4, the current territorial distribution of independent countries is increasingly frozen within existing borders, which have become sanctified in the legal doctrine of *uti possidetis juris* and can only be lawfully changed with the consent of all sovereign states involved (Ratner 1996, Shaw 1996).

Sovereign statehood, however, does not entail a permanently fixed domestic arrangement of political life. On the contrary, there are many possibilities, and sovereign states, particularly long-lasting ones, usually experience substantial reincarnations over the course of their history. Most European democracies previously were monarchies. Some now are constitutional monarchies – Britain, the Scandinavian and Benelux countries, Spain – under the effective control of democratic governments. All of them are welfare states of one kind or another. Some previous great powers (Spain, Sweden, the Netherlands) are today inconsequential good citizens of international society.

The successive reincarnations of Britain and the United States are indicative of the evolutionary nature of sovereign statehood domestically. Britain (formerly England) evolved from a royal tyranny under Henry VIII in the sixteenth century, to an absolutist monarchy under James I and Charles I, a quasi-dictatorship under Oliver Cromwell, and a restored monarchy with absolutist and pro-Catholic tendencies under Charles II and James II in the seventeenth century, to a parliamentary regime after the 'glorious revolution' of 1688–9, becoming from the eighteenth to the twentieth centuries the greatest overseas empire and the first fully industrialized country, a parliamentary democracy, a welfare state and no longer imperial power, and most recently a member of the European Union, prepared to pool some of its sovereignty with that of other EU states. Over the past two centuries the United States transformed itself from a small Atlantic seaboard republic of a slave-holding, ex-colonial bourgeoisie in the late eighteenth century, to an integrated, immigrant-populated, liberal society as well as a continent-straddling and industrializing giant in the nineteenth century, to a world power and multiracial democracy by the mid-twentieth century, the pre-eminent nation-state on the planet and the most spectacular nation-building project of modern history. A remote peripheral country became, by some considerable distance, the most central and consequential power on earth. What the future evolution of these two countries will involve nobody can say. That there will be further reincarnations and adaptations would seem very likely in the light of their histories.

To sum up: monarchies have become democracies. Literate and educated citizenries have been formed. Populations have been shaped into peoples, knitted together by transportation and communications networks, political and military mobilization, public education, and the like (Deutsch and Foltz 1963). Parliaments have been elected by an ever widening and now universal franchise. Aristocratic and oligarchic political factions have become national political parties. Governments have learned to manage – after a fashion – the wealth of nations. A few states and in particular Britain in the nineteenth century and the United States in the twentieth century have even attempted to manage the international economy. Welfare states have been built. Modern science and technology has been applied in national governance no less than other spheres of life, which has multiplied the power and reach of the state, both domestically and internationally. The range of government policy and activity, the areas of government involvement with society, have been continuously enlarged and vastly enhanced. These changes, and others too numerous to mention, have taken place over the past several centuries.

But that new architecture and furniture of the state is built upon old foundations. The political world continues to be an anarchical system composed of independent countries. States are still sovereign in the jurisdictional sense that their bordered territories are spheres of authority exclusive to themselves. They continue to possess constitutional independence, which is the liberty to enact their own laws, to organize and control their own armed forces and police, to tax themselves, to create and manage their own currencies, to make their own domestic and foreign policies, to conduct diplomatic relations with foreign governments, to organize and join international organizations, and in short to govern themselves according to their own ideas, interests, and values (James 1986). The right to do that continues to be universally prized. There is no higher authority over those countries, no international government to speak of. The United Nations, for example, is a creature and servant of the states system, particularly the major powers, and not an authority above them. The *respublica* is national and is still far from being cosmopolitan. What some scholars refer to as international governance is not yet 'government' in the standard English definition, which signifies 'the action or manner of governing . . . ; the fact that (a person, etc.) governs'. No authority or agency yet exists that 'governs' the states of the world. Nor is there any sign that one might be established in the foreseeable future.

Presuppositions of a states system

In Western Europe . . . there has been growing social cohesion, growing interdependence among the people, growth of state power, increasing flexibility in its operation, increasing wealth and its better distribution, diffusion of culture among the masses, the softening of manners, perhaps the lessening of violence – everything that the Victorians believed was inevitable. If Sir Thomas More or Henry IV, let us say, were to return to England and France in 1960, it is not beyond plausibility that they would admit that their countries had moved domestically towards goals and along paths which they could approve. But if they contemplated the international scene, it is more likely that they would be struck by resemblances to what they remembered . . . The stage would have become much wider, the actors fewer, their weapons more alarming, but the play would be the same old melodrama. (Wight 1968: 26)

Some forty years ago a British scholar made this historical observation. The sovereign foundations of the states system are still recognizable as being more or less what they continuously have been for the past several centuries. We take it for granted that the surface of the earth is partitioned into territorially differentiated, independent countries, and we act accordingly. We assume international borders – what originally were military frontiers – are significant rather than trivial when we transit them. Indeed, they are more precisely defined and more closely monitored in the early twenty-first century than they were in the nineteenth century. Passport controls, for example, were looser and the state was only beginning to monopolize the right to issue passport documents and to restrict them to its own nationals (*History of U.K. Passports: An Overview*). We assume there is a discernable and recognizable government that is the highest political and legal authority in each country, and that those governments have or should have control of their territorial jurisdictions. We do not assume that the laws of our own country are applicable and enforceable in the foreign country we are visiting or in which we are residing. We assume the population of each country (excluding visitors and permanent foreign residents) is composed of citizens and that very few people are citizens of more than one country.

We assume there is no such thing as 'world citizenship' established and enforced by a competent supranational authority. If we lose our case in the Supreme Court we do not expect to make an appeal to a higher court – unless our country is a member of the Council of Europe and has subjected itself to the European Court of Human Rights in Strasbourg. Even in that special case, however, the Court is a creature of the European states which are responsible for setting it up and accepting its judgments. It is a higher judicial authority only for the Europe of those states and not for anyone else. We assume national governments deal with each other under normal circumstances in ways that reflect the sovereign status of both. If that fails to happen it calls for some justification or explanation. For a post-sovereign world to exist, these assumptions and others like them would have to be altered a great deal if not abandoned altogether. I see no compelling evidence of any such transformation.

The presuppositions of an evolving system of sovereign states can be interrogated, briefly, by several arguments that posit scenarios of transformation. The European Union is sometimes portrayed as 'a thoroughgoing transcendence of the sovereign state' (MacCormick 1996: 555). Since the late 1950s European states have been constructing and joining the Union, whose membership continues to grow as countries queue for admission, the EU extends across Europe, and its executive arm, the European Commission, gets involved in an ever-widening circle of economic, social, political, and even military affairs in the continent and beyond (*Europa: Portal of the European Union*). Yet in whatever ways it might make sense to conceive of the European Union as 'going beyond sovereignty' there would still be an external border around a politically integrated EU which would presumably increase in height to compensate for internal borders between EU member states coming down. The EU border and not the borders of Germany, France, Italy, Spain, etc. would be the relevant boundary for regulating and policing transborder traffic and transport in that part of the world. The international assumption of a border, of inside and outside a sovereign jurisdiction, would still apply. The prior sovereignty of the member states in respect of border transit and traffic would simply be transferred to the EU itself.

The European Union is the creature of its member states. It will flourish and evolve, perhaps into a European federation at some time in the future, if its member states and their citizens will that to happen and make it happen. Should that eventually happen – which is still only a possibility – the outcome will not mark an end to the states system in Europe. Rather, it will signal an important realignment of the system by reducing the number of sovereign states in the continent. The EU will become one large and very significant sovereign state, perhaps a new superpower, involved in a re-proportioned states system. A United States of Europe would be a momentous development in European affairs because it would domesticate the politics of a large part of the continent. That might be welcomed by Europeans and non-Europeans alike who know something of Europe's turbulent and violent international history. That would also be an important development in world affairs because it would alter, to some extent, the international landscape. The balance of power would perhaps have a major new balancer. But it would not signal even the slightest movement away from the global states system, which would still exist as completely as it exists today. A United States of Europe would be a member state of a world of sovereign states.

In another scenario, the United States is portrayed as an imperial or quasi-imperial state, operating in disregard of the states system when it is expedient to do so (Simes 2003). There is no doubting the worldwide influence of the United States, particularly the global reach of its military and commercial power. Many other states prudentially or astutely adapt their foreign policies, some even their domestic policies, to its global presence. But the United States does not govern foreign territories and populations as its imperial jurisdiction, like the European empires of previous centuries or the Roman Empire of antiquity (Canning 1996: 29–43). In its heyday the British Empire exercised sovereign authority over numerous dependencies around the world, which comprised about a quarter of the world's population and land mass. In order to become constitutionally independent Canada, Australia, New Zealand, South Africa, India, Pakistan, Nigeria, Malaya,

Jamaica, and every other former British dependency had to obtain a transfer of sovereignty from Great Britain. The United States does not exercise sovereignty over any other country, apart from a few minor dependencies. Nor does it seek to acquire sovereign control of other places. That is not because such control is unimportant. It is because the United States by and large respects the sovereignty of countries around the world, and only trespasses when its vital interests and concerns are deemed to be at stake. To that end, the United States seeks to align as many independent states as possible with its goals, its values, and its policies. It has been doing that on a global basis since 1945 and with considerable success, although never complete success. Some countries refuse or resist being aligned with the United States, particularly substantial powers with a self-conception of their own centrality in world affairs – such as Russia, China, and even France from time to time. That, too, is only to be expected in a world of sovereign states.

Turning to a related scenario, it is often said that the United States today is the vanguard of an international movement to establish democracy as the only legitimate form of government around the world. US foreign policy has proclaimed the goal of spreading democracy. A chorus of Western leaders have repeated the refrain. American presidents, beginning with Woodrow Wilson, have declared the urgency of making the world 'safe for democracy' (Wilson 1917). A few have gone so far as to wage wars whose aims have included 'regime change' in pursuit of democracy: wars in Kosovo, Afghanistan, and of course 'Operation Iraqi Freedom'. Even if democracy were to become the basis of international legitimacy, however, the states system would still be a plural world of self-determining and self-governing states. The outcome patently would not be one cosmopolitan democracy. Washington would not become the capital of the world. States would not be any less sovereign for being democracies. The doctrines and practices of popular sovereignty would merely be more widespread than they are at present.

In yet another scenario – which develops a previous point – it is often claimed that the political world is being transformed by proliferating non-state actors and non-governmental organizations, indeed to such an extent that sovereign states are being undermined (Boli and Thomas 1999). This argument does correctly draw our attention to transnational activities and networks which are expanding at a rapid rate and now constitute an important feature of the international scene. But any claim that a world of such actors and organizations is displacing the system of sovereign states – rather than merely operating under their jurisdiction and protection – is misleading. Globalization presupposes the existence of the system of states. The states system opens and secures a space for transnational activity, making it feasible to conduct operations and engage in transactions on an international plane. Non-state actors and organizations operate within that system, and not outside it. They operate under the conditions of peace and security that the states system alone brings into existence. I say 'alone' because it is still the case that sovereign states and the great powers in particular, both individually and jointly, carry the heavy responsibility for arranging and sustaining international order which at base is a diplomatic and military enterprise. Non-state actors and organizations are not responsible and could not be made responsible for that. In the absence of that underlying condition, they would face great operational hazards and difficulties and it would not be an exaggeration to suppose they might not be able to operate at all.

That raises the question of the relationship of the states system to world markets and transnational activities generally. Do international markets produce peace? Or is peace conducive to international trade and commerce, international travel and tourism, and other transnational activities? The history of war is indicative of an answer that is difficult to set aside. During wars international business activity goes to ground in areas affected by the conflict. Transport is interrupted and disrupted. Insurance lapses or the cost becomes prohibitive. Travel and tourism collapse when people stay home. One of the better-established propositions of world politics is: during periods of international disorder and conflict, especially war, among the first casualties are cross-border activities, personal, commercial, scientific, educational, cultural, and other. Insofar as such activities constitute an international civil society, it too is dependent on the states system.

This argument can be made another way. All private organizations, including large multinational business enterprises, are lacking the crucial means – territory and sovereignty – to operate completely on their own. It would be impossible for Microsoft or Toyota or British Petroleum to engage in business activities in different parts of the world without the permission and protection of particular states whose territorial jurisdictions they necessarily must operate from. Even if business enterprises use their economic clout to open the doors of independent states by supplying business investment or bribing rulers they still do not possess the sovereign keys that unlock them. Sovereign states alone hold those keys. That is the necessary condition in the entire arrangement: states are sovereign and multinational or transnational organizations are dependent on their sovereignty. If international order can be said to exist, it is because the states system, especially the great powers, make it a reality. It does not happen automatically. Adam Smith's invisible hand of the free market (Smith 1994) is ultimately dependent on the mailed fist of the sovereign state.

Business firms, religious confessions and denominations, humanitarian organizations, scientific bodies, artistic associations, environmental activists, international sporting activities, academic conferences, and almost any other transnational actor or activity that one could identify – all are dependent upon the international order that can only be established and sustained by the states system. Non-state actors are riders and some are free riders on that system. When academics fly at 30,000 feet in B777s or A340s to international conferences around the world, it is sovereign states and the intergovernmental and non-governmental organizations supported by them that make it possible. Airports are parts of territorial sovereignty. Airspace is subject to regulatory control by sovereign states and their agents. We fly in confidence and safety without giving much thought, if any, to that worldwide and state-based arrangement (Thirty Thousand Feet: Aviation Directory). Globalization theorists do the same.

This brings us back to where the chapter began: the issue of terrorism and the sovereign state. Terrorists are non-state actors. From that conceptualization, however, it is sometimes argued that terrorist activities undermine the states system by challenging the authority and power of sovereign states: that is by combating their police and military power, by testing their constitutional and legal orders, and generally by provoking public alarm and political consternation about the safety of citizens and the security of the state. All that is undoubtedly true, but it can leave an erroneous impression that terrorism is beyond the world of sovereign states.

In their very designs, schemes, and actions terrorists predicate the sovereign state and states system, which is the relevant political and legal context within which terrorism is conceived. Terrorists attack states via their citizens to force their governments to change the course of foreign or domestic policy. Some terrorist groups, particularly separatists and irredentists, display state-like ambitions and pretensions: the Irish Republican Army and the Basque Homeland and Freedom Organization (ETA) are well-known examples. Or they have a political hubris that derives from challenging the authority and power of sovereign states: al-Qaeda against the United States: David and Goliath. The consequences of a terrorist attack may even warrant such pretensions. The tiny band of terrorists who attacked New York and Washington succeeded in provoking a response from the United States that arguably was out of all proportion to the event and the subsequent perceived threat. The course of American domestic and foreign policy was profoundly affected, although not in the way the terrorists perhaps hoped it would be. The subsequent anti-terrorist efforts and expenses have been huge. Wars have been launched in Afghanistan and Iraq, controversial anti-terrorist legislation has been enacted, government bureaucracies have been reorganized and government budgets realigned, and a huge financial deficit has resulted. The repercussions in domestic politics and international politics were still being felt at the time of writing.

Terrorism is an unlawful threat or use of violence in pursuit of political goals. Some definitions of terrorism include ideological or religious aims, but those are also clearly political in that they target citizens and governments of sovereign states. The UK Terrorism Act 2000 speaks of 'the use or threat' of terrorism taken 'for the purpose of advancing a political, religious or ideological cause' (ch. 11, pt. I). The word 'political' presupposes sovereign states as the basic units and agents of both international politics and domestic politics. Terrorists see themselves as 'soldiers' waging war for a great cause that is directed at an 'enemy', which almost invariably turns out to be the governments and citizens of sovereign states. Terrorists are not armed forces in the usual sense. Terrorists engage in a supposed warfare, and some states reinforce that impression by characterizing their response as 'war on terrorism'. But terrorists have no recognized rights to wage war, which is exclusively possessed by sovereign governments and by international organizations or other actors recognized by them. Their actual capacity to threaten and harm the citizens of states is small if not minuscule as compared to the security threat that states can present to each other – or to their own citizens when the government falls into the hands of tyrants and despots.

The terrorist attacks on New York and Washington were not only acts of violence against the civilian employees and employers in the Twin Towers or against the military and civilian personnel in the Pentagon. Nor were they attacks on the cities of New York and Washington. They were attacks on the United States of America, on its power and prestige, which the Twin Towers and the Pentagon symbolized. Everybody understood that. The al-Qaeda attackers were seeking to effect a change in particular foreign policies of the United States toward the Middle East. Terrorists exploit the physical vulnerability and anxiety of citizens, via the furious media reaction to their attacks, and the consequent dismay of the government, for the express purpose of changing the foreign and domestic policies of the targeted state. That is what Islamic terrorists apparently succeeded in accomplishing by their 2004 attack on packed commuter trains in Madrid. It was followed by a change of government and the withdrawal of Spanish forces from the American-led war on terrorism in Iraq.

Terrorism postulates state sovereignty but it presents legal difficulties, particularly as regards the lawful options of sovereign states in responding to such violence. A threat or act of violence against civilians that has no political cause could be construed, prima facie, as an exclusively criminal act. The agents of terrorism, however, are not clearly and unambiguously criminals. Yet neither are they soldiers whose terrible activities can readily be labelled as war crimes. Terrorist violence is also to be distinguished from internationally recognized forms of armed activity by non-state actors, such as wars of national liberation against colonial powers. Terrorist violence is neither criminal violence nor the lawful exercise of armed force. Therein resides the perplexing ambiguity of terrorism in a world of sovereign states which, for most purposes, are understood to possess exclusive rights of waging war. That is the focal point of the controversy as to whether terrorists, when they are captured, should be treated as prisoners of war and possibly charged with committing war crimes, or treated as criminals and charged under criminal codes, or dealt with in some other manner. Yet in whatever way that issue may be decided when it is confronted in any particular case, it can be determined entirely from within the political and legal framework of state sovereignty.

Terrorism involves sovereign states in a more direct and immediate fashion when such states provide locations or sanctuaries, financial aid, military assistance, and in some cases even direct operational assistance to terrorists. It is regrettable but surely not surprising that some terrorists operate with the indulgence or even the assistance of sovereign states, which presumably have their policy reasons for extending such toleration or support. Terrorist organizations must locate and operate on sovereign territory somewhere. They may be obliged to do that in secret where the government does not tolerate terrorism and tries to suppress it. Some governments may not be prepared to suppress terrorists that are operating on or from their territory. Some governments may not be able to suppress them. That may present serious difficulties to other countries if the terrorists are attacking their citizens from such bases: the evident problem of Israel in dealing with attacks by Hezbollah terrorists launched from the territory of Lebanon (Harik 2005). Some governments may harbour terrorists. Some governments may use terrorist organizations as a means to their own political ends. Some governments may even engage in 'terrorist' activities via organizations they establish or co-opt for that purpose. Some terrorist organizations may be so dependent on the assistance of such governments, and so involved with them, that they become their 'puppets': state-sponsored terrorism.

Sovereign states that harbour, nurture, or manipulate terrorists – even states that may be unable to suppress terrorists operating on or from their territory – are placing themselves outside the legitimate international system and its legal protections and immunities. They are threatening or acquiescing in a threat to other sovereign states and to the international order. They are in breach of international law. They are provoking foreign powers to intervene in their territorial jurisdiction or to take other actions to deal with the threat. All of that is intelligible in the context of sovereign states and the states system, domestic law and international law. Indeed, it is only intelligible in that context.

The United Kingdom Terrorism Act 2000 has a definition of 'terrorism' that conveys the conception that it is unlawful violence against the state and its citizens, and that it involves the states system and not only the targeted state (ch. 11, pt. I). According to that legislation, terrorist action is 'designed to influence the government or to intimidate the public or a section of the public'. It is taken 'for the purpose of advancing a political, religious or ideological cause'. It 'involves serious violence against a person' or 'endangers a person's life'. It 'creates a serious risk to the health or safety of the public or a section of the public'. It involves 'serious damage to property'. The Act makes a point of emphasizing that terrorism 'includes action outside the United Kingdom', that it 'is a reference to any person, or to property, wherever situated', regardless of international boundaries. In the act 'the public includes a reference to the public of a country other than the United Kingdom,' and ' "the government" means the government of the United Kingdom, of a Part of the United Kingdom or of a country other than the United Kingdom.' Here is a legal statement by a major state with extensive experience of terrorism, both domestic and international, which explicitly indicates that sovereign states and their citizens, and the states system at large, are the relevant context in which terrorism ought to be understood and combatted.

Between past and future

Even when we put our minds to the task it is not easy to think about world affairs in a down-to-earth way without employing the ideas and language associated with state sovereignty, which are deeply ingrained in human affairs (Jackson 2000a: 421). It is difficult to come up with a realistic alternative *Weltanschauung*. That surely is because of 'the tyranny of the concepts' associated with the sovereign state which constitute an intellectual prison from which an escape, which is not merely a flight of fancy, is anything but easy (Bull 1971: ch. 11). That may assign too much importance to the intellectual aspect, however, insofar as the states system is so completely a part of our existential world, our unreflective everyday lives, that it is easy to conform to it without giving it much thought – in rather the same way that other fundamental and long-lasting arrangements for ordering and conducting human affairs are taken for granted or assumed without reflection when making use of them.

It may be worthwhile to call attention to the enduring place of some of the many contrivances and techniques that people have come up with for arranging and easing their individual and collective lives: calendars, clocks, compasses, books, maps, tools and utensils, cooking recipes, musical instruments and notation, numeric notation, units of measure, geometry and algebra, alphabets, signals and signs, to mention a few. There are also many examples of the longevity and adaptability of practices, institutions, and rules over the course of centuries: long-standing games such as chess and cards or cricket and baseball, religious and political rituals, marriage and the family, the church, mosque, and temple, national anthems, elementary education and particularly the teaching of literacy, the college and university system including departments of knowledge such as philosophy or medicine or physics or theology, the institution of private property, money and banking, hospices and hospitals, the law of contracts, rules of precedence and procedure, parliamentary rules of order, practices of diplomacy, hierarchical ranks and units of armed forces, among many others.

These arrangements for the conduct of human affairs have remained recognizably the same in spite of profound social changes. That is because they provide something elementary: stable, familiar, and convenient modalities of social expectation, interaction, and cooperation. They enable people to keep their bearings on the stormy seas set in motion by their own wave-making activities, which generate historical change.

People hold on to conventional ways of arranging and conducting their affairs in the various departments of human life, each generation passes them on to the next generation, and the cycle repeats itself over and over. That should make us sceptical about claims that world affairs are getting beyond sovereign statehood. Instead, it suggests that continuity and change often march hand in hand.

There is nothing that is inevitable or sacrosanct about the sovereign states system. It is a human arrangement from start to finish, meaning it is historical. It could change fundamentally. It could disappear just as the Roman Empire disappeared and Latin Christendom disappeared. Such an episode would obviously mark a world-historical transformation. It still remains to be seen whether the sovereign states system will adapt successfully to the scientific, technological, economic, and social changes that we summarize by the term 'globalization'. It could conceivably bleed to death from a thousand small cuts of non-state actors. But where will that leave them? Where will they turn for performance and accountability in matters that involve the swords of war and peace, of crime and punishment, if they cannot perform those fundamental public services themselves and assuming that some people or groups will still pose a threat to others – as seems entirely likely?

The evolution of that system over the past three or four centuries, the fact that it proved to have a comparative advantage over all existing systems it encountered, the fact that no new system came into existence that could displace it, the fact that there is no realistic and practical alternative even on the horizon and that the only conceivable alternatives remain pinned to academic drawing boards – all of that inclines me to believe that the sovereign states system will continue to evolve in the foreseeable future as it has in the historical past. We clearly are no longer at the beginning of modern history, but it is far from certain that we are near the end, or that we have entered a post-sovereign era. If we are living in a world that some among us would label as post-modern, it is not a world that is likely to abandon state sovereignty any time soon.

Notes

Note to preface

1 'State' is the proper name for those organizations in international law. Most of the world uses the word in that way. Americans prefer 'nations' to distinguish sovereign 'states' from the states of the United States. But 'nation' is more ambiguous. Most 'nations' are not sovereign although many, such as Quebec, Scotland, and Chechnya, may harbour a desire for national independence.

Note to chapter 1

1 For a view of sovereignty as a far older idea, see Hinsley (1966: 27–45).

Note to chapter 2

1 Somewhat similar tensions still arise in the modern Catholic Church between the pope and curia in Rome and national assemblies of Catholic clergy, such as the United States Conference of Catholic Bishops.

Notes to chapter 3

1 Italy remained a regional sub-system of city-states, periodically conquered or occupied by great powers, until the mid-nineteenth century when a unified Italian nation-state was finally created.
2 The Holy Roman Empire survived formally until 1806 when it was dissolved during the Napoleonic Wars.

3 Thomas Hobbes famous book on the subject, *Leviathan*, was published in 1651.

Notes to chapter 6

1 In the interests of free trade, the Corn Laws were repealed in 1846 and the Navigation Acts in 1847 and 1854. See *A Web of English History*: http://www.historyhome.co.uk/ and *Encyclopaedia Britannica Online*: http://www.britannica.com/eb/article-9055084

2 Current international law on piracy is located in the *United Nations Convention on the Law of the Sea*, Art. 101. Also see 'Regional Cooperation Agreement on Combating Piracy', *American Society of International Law*, May 2005: http://www.asil. org/ilib/2005/05/ilib050509.htm#t3

References

Ackroyd, P. (1999). *The Life of Thomas More*. New York: Anchor Books.

Alexandrowicz, C. (1969). 'New and Original States', *International Affairs*, 45/3: 465–80.

Allen, J. (1977). *A History of Political Thought in the Sixteenth Century*. London: Methuen.

Anti-Slavery Society (2006): http://www.anti-slaverysociety.addr. com/slavery.htm

Armitage, D. (2005). 'The Contagion of Sovereignty: Declarations of Independence since 1776', *South African Historical Journal Online*: http://www.journals.co.za/ej/ejour_sahist.html

Armstrong, D. (1998). 'Globalization and the Social State', *Review of International Studies*, 24: 461–78.

Bain, W. (2003). *Between Anarchy and Society*. Oxford: Oxford University Press.

Barker, E. (1956). *Principles of Social and Political Theory*. Oxford: Oxford University Press.

Barker, E. (1963). *Political Thought in England*. Oxford: Oxford University Press.

Bartlett, R. (1993). *The Making of Europe*. Harmondsworth: Penguin Books.

Berlin, I. (1992). *The Crooked Timber of Humanity*. New York: Vintage Books.

Bloch, M. (1964). 'Social Classes and Political Organization', in *Feudal Society*, vol. 2. Chicago: University of Chicago Press.

Bodin, Jean (1955). *Six Books of the Commonwealth*, abridged and translated by M. J. Tooley. Oxford: Basil Blackwell.

Boli, J. and G. Thomas (1999). *Constructing World Culture: Non-governmental Organizations since 1875*. Stanford: Stanford University Press.

Booth, K. (1995). 'Human Wrongs and International Relations,' *International Affairs*, 71: 103–26.

Brierly, J. (1936). *The Law of Nations*, 2nd edn. London: Oxford University Press.

Brownlie, I. (1979). *Principles of Public International Law*, 3rd edn. Oxford: Clarendon Press, 1979.

Bull, H. (1971). *The Anarchical Society*. London: Macmillan.

Bull, H. and A. Watson (1984). *The Expansion of International Society*. Oxford: Clarendon Press.

Burckhardt, J. (1992). *The Civilization of the Renaissance in Italy*. New York: Barnes & Noble.

Burgi, N. and P. Golub (2000). 'Has Globalisation Really Made Nations Redundant?' *Le Monde Diplomatique* http://www.globalpolicy.org/nations/global.htm

Bury, J. (1967). *The Invasion of Europe by the Barbarians*. New York: Norton.

Cairns, H. A. (1965). *Prelude to Imperialism*. London: Routledge.

Cameron, E. (1991). *The European Reformation*. Oxford: Clarendon Press.

Canning, J. (1996). *A History of Medieval Political Thought*. London: Routledge.

Carroll, L. (1991). *Through the Looking Glass*. Electronic version of Millennium Fulcrum edition: http://www.cs.indiana.edu/metastuff/looking/looking.txt.gz

Catholic Encyclopedia Online ed. K. Knight. At http://www.newadvent.org/cathen/index.html

Cicero (1950). *The Republic*. Boston: Loeb Classical Library.

Clark, G. (1960). *The Seventeenth Century*. New York: Oxford University Press.

Cobban, A. (1939). *Dictatorship*. New York: Charles Scribners.

Collinson, P. (1993). 'The Late Medieval Church and its Reformation: 1400–1600', in J. McManners (ed.), *The Oxford History of Christianity*. Oxford: Clarendon Press, 243–76.

Connolly, W. (1987). *Politics and Ambiguity*. Madison: University of Wisconson Press.

Cooper, R. (2002). 'The Postmodern State': http://observer.guardian.co.uk/worldview/story/0,11581,680095,00.html

Darby, H. and H. Fullard (eds) (1979). *The New Cambridge Modern History Atlas*. Cambridge: Cambridge University Press.

Del Rosso Jr., S. (1995). 'The Insecure State (What Future for the State)?' *Daedalus*, 124/2: 175–207.

D'Entrèves, A. (1939). *The Medieval Contribution to Political Thought*. Oxford: Oxford University Press.

D'Entrèves, A. (1970). *Natural Law*. London: Hutchinson.

Deutsch, K. and W. Foltz (eds) (1963). *Nation-Building*. New York: Atherton Press.

Dicey, A. V. (1956). *Law of the Constitution*. London: Macmillan.

DUPI (Danish Institute of International Affairs) (1999). *Humanitarian Intervention: Legal and Political Aspects*. Copenhagen: Nordisk Bog Center.

Durham, Lord (1839). *Report On the Affairs of British North America*. Documents in Quebec History: http://www2.marianopolis.edu/quebechistory/docs/durham/1.htm

Elliott, J. (1992). 'A Europe of Composite Monarchies', *Past and Present*, 137: 48–71.

Encyclopaedia Britannica Online: http://www.britannica.com/eb/article-9055084

Europa: Portal of the European Union: http://europa.eu.int/

Evans, G. and M. Sahnoun (2001). *The Responsibility to Protect: Report of the International Commission on Intervention and State Sovereignty*. Ottawa: International Development Research Centre.

Figgis, J. (1965). *The Divine Right of Kings*. New York: Harper Torchbooks.

Finley, M. (1983). *Politics in the Ancient World*. Cambridge: Cambridge University Press.

Fletcher, R. (1998). *The Conversion of Europe*. London: Fontana.

Friedrich, C. (1963). *The Philosophy of Law in Historical Perspective*. Chicago: University of Chicago Press.

Fukuyama, F. (1991). 'Liberal Democracy as a Global Phenomenon', *PS: Political Science and Politics*, 24/4: 659–64.

Ganshof, F. (1964). *Feudalism*, tr. P. Grierson. London: Longmans.

Gellner, E. (1993). *Nations and Nationalism*. Oxford: Blackwell.

Gierke, O. (1987). *Political Theories of the Middle Age*. Cambridge: Cambridge University Press.

Gong, G. (1984). *The Standard of 'Civilization' in International Society*. Oxford: Clarendon Press.

Grimm, H. (1948). 'Luther's Conception of Territorial and National Loyalty', *Church History*, 17/2: 79–94.

Grotius, H. (2005). *The Freedom of the Seas*. The Online Library of Liberty, Liberty Fund: http://oll.libertyfund.org/Home3/Book.php?recordID=0049

Gustafsson, H. (1998). 'The Conglomerate State: A Perspective on State Formation in Early Modern Europe', *Scandinavian Journal of History*, 23/3–4: 189–213.

Hannaford, I. (1996). *Race: The History of an Idea in the West*. Baltimore: Johns Hopkins University Press.

Harik, J. (2005). *Hezbollah*. London: Tauris Publishers.

Hartdegen, S. (1970). *The New American Bible*. New York: Thomas Nelson.

Held, D. (1995). *Democracy and the Global Order*. Stanford: Stanford University Press.

Held, D. (2004). *A Globalizing World?* London: Routledge.

Henckaerts, J. (1995). *Mass Expulsion in Modern International Law and Practice*. The Hague: Martinus Nijhoff.

Hill, B. W. (1975). *Edmund Burke: On Government, Politics and Society*. Brighton, Sussex: Harvester Press.

Himmelfarb, G. (1962). *Lord Acton: A Study in Conscience and Politics*. Chicago: University of Chicago Press.

Hinsley, F. H. (1966). *Sovereignty*. Cambridge: Cambridge University Press.

Hinsley, F. H. (1967). *Power and the Pursuit of Peace*. Cambridge: Cambridge University Press.

History of U.K. Passports: An Overview. United Kingdom, Home Office: http://www.ukpa.gov.uk/index.asp

Hobbes, T. (1946). *Leviathan*, ed. M. Oakeshott. Oxford: Basil Blackwell.

Hobbes, T. (1993). *Man and Citizen (De Homine and De Cive)*, ed. B. Gert. Indianapolis: Hackett.

Hudson, C. E. (1947). 'The Church and International Affairs', *International Affairs*, 23/1: 1–10.

ICRC (International Committee for the Red Cross) (2006). *International Humanitarian Law and Human Rights*. At http://www.icrc.org/Web/eng/siteeng0.nsf/htmlall/section_ihl_and_human_rights

International Maritime Bureau: http://www.icc-ccs.org/imb/overview.php

Jackson, R. (1990). *Quasi-States: Sovereignty, International Relations, and the Third World*. Cambridge: Cambridge University Press.

Jackson, R. (2000a). *The Global Covenant: Human Conduct in a World of States*. Oxford: Oxford University Press.

Jackson, R. (2000b). 'Humanitarian War over Kosovo', *Politica*, 32: 23–47.

Jackson Preece, J. (1998a). *National Minorities and the European Nation-States System*. Oxford: Clarendon Press.

Jackson Preece, J. (1998b). 'Multiculturalism, Dignity and the Liberal State in Canada', *Politica*, 30/2: 149–67.

Jackson Preece, J. (1998c). 'Ethnic Cleansing as an Instrument of Nation-State Creation', *Human Rights Quarterly*, 20/4: 817–42.

Jackson Preece, J. (2005). *Minority Rights: Between Diversity and Community*. Cambridge: Polity.

James I, King of England (1609). 'On the Divine Right of Kings', Extracts from a Speech to Parliament (21 March 1609), at http://staff.gps.edu/mines/Age%20of%20Absolu-%20James%20I%20on%20Divine%20Rights.htm

James, A. (1986). *Sovereign Statehood: The Basis of International Society*. London: Allen & Unwin.

James, S. (1989). 'The Myth of the People', *Reviews in American History*, 17: 182–6.

Johnson, D. (1957). 'Piracy in Modern International Law', *Transactions of the Grotius Society*, 43: 63–85.

Kant, E. (2006). *Groundwork for the Metaphysics of Morals*. At http://www.msu.org/ethics/content_ethics/texts/kant/kanttxt3.html#com1

Kantorowicz, E. (1957). *The King's Two Bodies*. Princeton: Princeton University Press.

Keen, M. (1991). *The History of Medieval Europe*. Harmondsworth: Penguin Books.

Kenerman, G. and P. Resnick (eds) (2005). *Insiders and Outsiders: Alan Cairns and the Reshaping of Canadian Citizenship*. Vancouver: University of British Columbia Press.

Knowles, D. (1967). 'Church and State in Christian History', *Journal of Contemporary History*, 2/4: 3–15.

Knowles, D. (1979). *The Religious Orders in England*. Cambridge: Cambridge University Press.

Krasner, S. (1999). *Sovereignty: Organized Hypocrisy*. Princeton: Princeton University Press.

Krieger, L. (ed.) (1967). 'Beginning of the Modern State', in *Lord Acton: Essays in the Liberal Interpretation of History*. Chicago: University of Chicago Press.

Lively, J. (1975). *Democracy*. Oxford: Basil Blackwell.

Lloyd, T. (1984). *The British Empire*. Oxford: Oxford University Press.

Locke, J. (1965). *Two Treatises of Government*. New York: Mentor.

MacCormick, N. (1996). 'Liberalism, Nationalism and the Post-Sovereign State', *Political Studies*, 44: 553–67.

Machiavelli, N. (1961). *The Prince*, tr. and ed. G. Bull. Harmondsworth: Penguin Books.

McIlwain, C. H. (1932). *The Growth of Political Thought in the West*. New York: Macmillan.

Macpherson, C. B. (1965). *The Real World of Democracy*. Oxford: Oxford University Press.

Maitland, F. (1979). *The Constitutional History of England*. Cambridge: Cambridge University Press.

Mathew, D. (1948). *Catholicism in England: Portrait of a Minority*. London: Eyre & Spottiswoode.

Mattingly, G. (1962). *The Armada*. Boston: Houghton Mifflin.

Mattingly, G. (1988). *Renaissance Diplomacy*. New York: Dover Publications.

Mayall, J. (1990). *Nationalism and International Society*. Cambridge: Cambridge University Press.

Mayr-Harting, H. (1993). 'The West: The Age of Conversion', in J. McManners (ed.), *The Oxford History of Christianity*. Oxford: Oxford University Press.

Mazrui, A. (1967). *Towards a Pax Africana*. Chicago. University of Chicago Press.

Mead, S. (1967). 'The "Nation with the Soul of a Church"', *Church History*, 36/3: 262–83.

Mill, J. S. (2000). 'Nationality', 391–8, in *Utilitarianism, On Liberty, Considerations on Representative Government*. London: Dent-Everyman's Library.

Mises, L. von (1983). *Nation, State and Economy*. New York: New York University Press.

Morgan, E. (1988). *Inventing the People: The Rise of Popular Sovereignty in England and America*. New York: W.W. Norton.

Morrall, J. (1958). *Political Thought in Medieval Times*. London: Hutchinson.

Nicholas, B. (1987). *An Introduction to Roman Law*. Oxford: Clarendon Press.

Nicolson, H. (1945). *Peacemaking 1919*. London: Constable.

'North Atlantic Treaty, Article 5', The Avalon Project at Yale Law School: http://www.yale.edu/lawweb/avalon/nato.htm#art5

Oakeshott, M. (1939). *The Social and Political Doctrines of Contemporary Europe*. Cambridge: Cambridge University Press.

Oakeshott, M. (1975). 'The Vocabulary of the Modern European State', *Political Studies*, 23: 319–41, 409–314.

Oakeshott, M. (1991). *Rationalism in Politics and Other Essays*. New and Expanded Edition. Indianapolis: Liberty Press.

Osiander, A. (1994). *The States System of Europe, 1640–1990*. New York: Oxford University Press.

Oxford English Dictionary Online (OED) (2006). At http://dictionary.oed.com/.htm.

Paine, T. (1985). *Rights of Man*. Baltimore: Penguin Classics.

Parry, J. (1966). *Europe and a Wider World*. London: Hutchinson.

Pastor, L. (1901). *The History of the Popes*, vol. 6. London: Kegan Paul.

Pellet, A. (1982). 'The Opinions of the Badinter Arbitration Committee', *European Journal of International Law*, 3: 178–85.

Pennington, K. (1970). 'Bartolomé de Las Casas and the Tradition of Medieval Law', *Church History*, 39/2: 149–61.

Philpott, D. (2001). *Revolutions in Sovereignty*. Princeton: Princeton University Press.

Pollard, A. (1948). *Factors in Modern History*. London: Constable.

Ratner, S. (1996). 'Drawing a Better Line: *Uti Possidetis* and the Borders of New States', *American Journal of International Law*, 90: 590–624.

'Regional Cooperation Agreement on Combating Piracy', The American Society of International Law, May 2005: http://www.asil.org/ilib/2005/05/ilib050509.htm#t3

Reiss, H. (ed.) (1991). *Kant: Political Writings*, 2nd edn. Cambridge: Cambridge University Press.

Ritter, G. (1976). *Frederick the Great*, ed. Peter Paret. Berkeley: University of California Press.

Roberts, A. and R. Guelff (eds) (1989). *Documents on the Laws of War*, 2nd edn. Oxford: Clarendon Press.

Rotberg, R. (2002). 'The New Nature of Nation State Failure', *Washington Quarterly*, 25/3: 85–96.

Rousseau, J. J. (1988). *The Social Contract and Discourses*. London: Dent-Everyman's Library.

Rubin, A. (1998). *The Law of Piracy*. New York: Transnational Publishers.

Ruskola, T. (2005). 'Canton is not Boston: The Invention of American Imperial Sovereignty', *American Quarterly*, 57/3: 859–84.

Salamon, L., S. Sokolowski, and R. List (2003). *Global Civil Society: An Overview*. Baltimore: Johns Hopkins University Institute for Policy Studies: http://www.jhu.edu/~ccss/pubs/pdf/globalciv.pdf

Schechtman, J. (1946). *European Population Transfers 1939–1945*. Oxford: Oxford University Press.

Schultz, G. (2002). Televised speech, C-SPAN Television, Washington DC, March 17.

Scruton, R. (1996). *A Dictionary of Political Thought*. London: Macmillan.

Seed, P. (1993). 'Are These Not Also Men?' *Journal of Latin American Studies*, 25/3: 629–52.

Shaw, M. (1996). 'The Heritage of States: The Principle of *Uti Possidetis Juris* Today', *British Yearbook of International Law*, 67: 75–154.

Shennan, J. (1974). *The Origins of the Modern European State*. London: Hutchinson.

Simes, D. (2003). 'America's Imperial Dilemma', *Foreign Affairs*, 82/6: 91–102.

Skinner, Q. (1978). *The Foundations of Modern Political Thought*, vol. 2. *The Age of Reformation*. Cambridge: Cambridge University Press.

Smith, A. (1994). *The Wealth of Nations*. New York: Random House.

Spengler, R. and J. (1964). *Tradition, Values and Socio-economic Development*. Durham, NC: Duke University Press.

Stola, D. (1992). 'Forced Migrations in Central European History', *Instytut Historii*, 26/2: 324–41.

'Supplementary Convention on the Abolition of Slavery, the Slave Trade, and Institutions and Practices Similar to Slavery'. United Nations High Commissioner for Human Rights: http://www.ohchr.org/english/law/slavetrade.htm

Talmon, J. (1970). *The Origins of Totalitarian Democracy*. New York: Norton.

'Terrorism: Questions and Answers', Council on Foreign Relations: http://cfrterrorism.org/home/

'Terrorist Attacks Redefine Common Wisdom about Transatlantic Security', Center for Defense Information: http://www.cdi.org/terrorism/awacs.cfm

Thirty Thousand Feet, Aviation Directory: http://www.thirtythousandfeet.com/regulato.htm

Tocqueville, Alexis de (1955). *The Old Regime and the French Revolution*. Garden City, NY: Anchor Books.

Tocqueville, Alexis de (1960). *Democracy in America*, 2 vols. New York: Vintage Books.

United Kingdom Terrorism Act 2000. Queen's Printer of Acts of Parliament: http://www.opsi.gov.uk/Acts/acts2000/00011-b.htm#1

United Nations Charter: http://www.un.org/aboutun/charter/

United Nations Convention on the Law of the Sea: http://www.un.org/Depts/los/convention_agreements/texts/unclos/unclos_e.pdf

United Nations Convention against Transnational Organized Crime, UN Crime and Drug Conventions (United Nations: Office on Drugs and Crime): http://www.unodc.org/unodc/en/drug_and_crime_conventions.html

United Nations Report of the High-level Panel on Threats, Challenges and Change (2004): http://www.un.org/secureworld/

United States Patriot Act of Congress: http://www.epic.org/privacy/terrorism/hr3162.html

Universal Declaration of Human Rights (1948). United Nations Office of the High Commissioner for Human Rights: http://www.unhchr.ch/html/intlinst.htm]

Viorst, M. (ed.) (1994). 'The Act of Supremacy', in *The Great Documents of Western Civilization*. New York: Barnes & Noble: 97–8.

Web of English History, A: http://www.historyhome.co.uk/

Webster's Seventh New Collegiate Dictionary (1967). Springfield, Mass.: Merriam Company.

Wedgwood, C. V. (1964). *The Trial of Charles I*. Harmondsworth: Penguin Books.

Wheeler, N. (2000). *Saving Strangers*. Oxford: Oxford University Press.

Wight, M. (1952). *British Colonial Constitutions*. Oxford: Clarendon Press.

Wight, M. (1968). 'Why is there no International Theory?', in H. Butterfield and M. Wight (eds), *Diplomatic Investigations*. Cambridge, Mass.: Harvard University Press.

Wight, M. (1977). *Systems of States*. London: Leicester University Press.

Wilson, Woodrow (1917). 'President Woodrow Wilson's War Message', 65th Cong., 1st Sess. Senate Doc. No. 5, Serial No. 7264, Washington, DC, 1917; pp. 3–8, *passim*: http://www.lib.byu.edu/~rdh/wwi/1917/wilswarm.html

Wilson, Woodrow (1918). 'President Woodrow Wilson's Fourteen Points', The Avalon Project at Yale Law School: http://www.yale.edu/lawweb/avalon/wilson14.htm.

Wood, J. (1967). 'Christianity and the State', *Journal of the American Academy of Religion*, 35/3: 257–70.

Index

absolutism 63–4, 84
Acton, Lord 66
Alexandrowicz, Charles 73
Anglo-Egyptian Sudan 8
assimilation 98, 101
Atlantic Charter 3
Augustine, St 40
Austria 64, 66
authority
　ideas ix

Badinter Commission 110
balance of power 53, 54, 55
Bangladesh 101
barbarian tribes 25, 26
Barker, Ernest 85–86
Berlin, Isaiah 132
bishoprics 32
Bismarck, Otto von, Chancellor
　98, 109
Bodin, Jean 38, 47
Britain (England, United
　Kingdom) xiii, 87
　Act of Annates 45
　Act of Appeals 45
　Act of Supremacy 2, 45–6
　British Dominions 70

British Empire 69–71, 152
British House of Commons
　56
British Foreign Jurisdiction
　Act 72
British India 4, 101
British North America 70
Civil War 58–9
Corn laws 142
East India Company 142,
　143
enfranchisement of women
　83
English Bill of Rights 119,
　126
Navigation Acts 142
Northern Ireland (Ulster)
　100–1
Reform Act 83
Reformation 45–47
Slavery Abolition Act 117
Terrorism Act 2000 156,
　159
Burckhardt, Jacob 4
Burke, Edmund 66, 86
Bush, George W. 135
Byzantine Empire 25

Calvin, Jean 44
Canada xiii, 4, 16–17, 98,
    102–3
Canada-United States
    relations 16–17
Canadian Charter of Rights
    and Freedoms 103
'first nations' 103
multicultural diversity 103
Catholic Church 38, 142
Catholicism 48
Charlemagne, emperor 27
Charles I, king 2, 58–9, 60
Charter of Paris for a New
    Europe 108
Chesterton, G.K. 81
China 7, 74, 153
Chinese empire 144
Chinese Revolution 96
Christendom xi, 7, 25, 27,
    32–5, 53, 57, 67, 69
Christian missionaries 142–3
'Church, the' 29, 39, 41
Church councils 40
    Council of Constance 40
Church of England 2, 39
Church and state 33, 47, 65
    'Allegory of the Two Swords'
        34, 44
    canon law 31–2
    civil law 31–2
    civil courts 32
    cujus regio, ejus religio 39,
        50, 104
    ecclesiastical courts 32
    Erastianism 65
    regna (regnum) 6, 25, 27,
        28, 32, 36, 44, 56, 63
    regnum Anglicana 26
    regnum Gallicum 26
    rex 56, 63
    rex est imperator in regno
        suo 7, 48, 52
    rex in regno suo est
        imperator regni sui 3

rex superiorem non
    recognoscens 45
sacerdotium 27, 36, 40, 44
Churchill, Winston 3, 16
Cicero 118
Colbert, Jean 64
Cold War 109, 131
Columbus, Christopher 69
communitates 29
    medieval City of London 29
Concert of Europe 50
concordats 41
conglomerate or composite
    states 106
congregatio fidelium 44
Congress of Vienna 64
Connelly, William 81
Constantine, Emperor 26, 27
Cromwell, Oliver 59
Czechoslovakia 4, 100

Dante Alighieri 36
Dayton Agreement 108
decolonization 146–7
democracy 87–93
    cosmopolitan 153
    Greek or Athenian 89–90
    liberal or constitutional
        88–89, 92, 93
    peoples or popular 89, 90
    totalitarian 93
    town hall 90
Denmark xiii, 28, 98
    Lutheran Church 39
    Reformation 45
d'Entrèves, A.P. 1
de Tocqueville, Alexis 79, 81,
    88, 95
Dicey, A.V. 84
divine right of kings 56, 57
dynasticism 64
    'dynastic idiom of
        international politics'
        64
    dynastic marriage 63

dynasty
　Habsburg 64
　Stuart 62
　Tudor 62

ecclesia 26, 27, 32
　ecclesium Anglicana 26, 29,
　　36
　ecclesium Gallicum 26, 29
Elizabeth I, Queen 62
ethnic cleansing 99, 102, 109,
　131
Europe 27, 35, 49, 50–1, 52
　Council of Europe 122
　international 49–50
　'liberty of Europe' 54
　national minorities 98,
　　100–1, 111
　nationalities 97, 98
European Convention for the
　　Protection of Human
　　Rights 126
European Court of Human
　　Rights 122,126, 151
European imperialism 67–8,
　　105, 106
European settlements and
　　'settler states' 105–6
European system of states 53,
　　54–55, 62, 66
European Union xiii, 4, 122,
　　151–2
　Conference on Yugoslavia
　　110
　United States of Europe 152

failed states 115, 131
Ferdinand and Isabella, King
　　and Queen 69
feudalism 30, 63
Filmer, Sir Robert 60
First World War 99, 106, 142
France 64, 65, 93, 94, 98,
　　153
　Alsace 105

constitution 93
Declaration of the Rights of
　　Man 120
French Empire 70
French Revolution 95, 96
Franco-Prussian War 105
Frederick II ('The Great'), King
　　65–66

Gellner, Ernest 106
Germany 97, 100, 102, 105
　East Germany and West
　　Germany 109
　Nazi atrocities 121
　Nazi Germany 122, 125
　unification 98, 109
globalization 135–61
　cosmopolitanism 139
　drug trafficking 141
　'global civil society' 140
　'global associational
　　revolution' 140–1
　global markets 139–40,
　　154–5
　history 142–4
　non-governmental
　　organizations and non-
　　state actors 153–4
　transnational uncivil society
　　141
　transnationalism 139
　'world citizenship' 151
globalization thesis 138–44
God 28, 30, 37, 40, 44, 56,
　　57, 58, 61, 62, 81, 84,
　　96, 116
great powers 55
Grotius, Hugo 71, 73
Gulf War 109

Hamilton, Alexander 18
Helsinki Final Act 108
Henry VIII, king 2, 37, 45–6,
　　57, 58
Hinsley, F.H. 50

Hobbes, Thomas 17, 38, 47, 60, 119
  'the safety of the people is the supreme law' 114
  'state of nature' 137
  'Sword of Justice' 17, 18, 121, 138
  'Sword of War' 17, 18, 121, 138
Holy Roman Emperor 28, 36, 52
human rights 114–34
  civil conditions and countries 120
  civil rights 120
  discourse 115–20
  European Convention for the Protection of Human Rights 126
  European Court of Human Rights 126
  human flourishing 121, 122–3
  human vulnerability 119, 120–21
  human wrongs 118
  humanitas et universitas 118
  international law 123–8
  non-governmental organizations 127–8
humanitarian intervention 128–34
  Humanitarian Intervention: Legal and Political Aspects 129
  Report of the International Commission on Intervention and State Sovereignty 129
  responsibilities of states 128–32
Hungary 100
Hussein, Saddam 133

India 4, 101
international boundaries 9, 107

uti possidetis juris 110, 111, 147
international law (law of nations) 55, 71–2, 73, 74, 107, 111
  Åland Islands dispute 108
  definition 123
  General Act of the Berlin Conference 75
  Geneva Conventions 125
  Hague Conventions 125
  human rights 123–28
  international human rights law 124–5
  international humanitarian law 124–5
  law of nations sovereignty 123
international order 111
Iraq 4, 110, 133
Ireland xiii, 100–1
irredentism 107
Italy 97

James I, King 57
Jefferson, Thomas 79

Kant, Immanuel 116, 117
Kenya xii
Kosovo 133
Kuwait 4

Lambton, John George, Earl of Durham
League of Nations
  covenant 107
  Mandates System 75–76
  national minorities guarantees 107–8
Lebanon 158
Lincoln, Abraham 79
Lively, Jack 91
Locke, John 60
'lordship' 28–9, 32
Louis XIV, king 2, 52, 54, 64, 66

Luther, Martin 38, 42
  theology of the godly prince
    44
Lutheranism 44

Machiavelli, Niccolò 38, 40,
  42
Macmillan, Harold 4
McIlwain, Charles 6
Madison, James 84
Marshall Plan 122
Marsiglio of Padua 36–7, 41,
  42
Mill, John Stuart 21, 90, 98
Mogul Empire 7, 146
More, Thomas, Lord
  Chancellor 46
multiculturalism 102
Mussolini, Benito 96

Napoleon Bonaparte 54, 65,
  93
natural law 73
Netherlands (Holland) 50
  Dutch East India Company
    142, 143
  Dutch Empire 69
  Dutch rebellion 58
  States-General ('Estates-
    General') 58, 61
Newfoundland 3
North Atlantic Treaty
  Organization (NATO)
  102, 109, 115, 122,
  133, 136
Northern Ireland xiii, 100–1

Oakeshott, Michael 85
Ottoman Empire 7, 25, 97,
  144
  Turkey 100

Paine, Thomas 78, 118, 119
  'natural rights' 118
Pakistan 4, 101
Palestine 101

papacy and popes 25, 27, 34,
  36, 40, 45–7, 50, 52,
  53, 58, 82
  Alexander VI 69
  Alexander VII 2, 52
  Bishop of Rome 36
  Innocent X 52
  Investiture Contest 27
  Leo III 27
  Vicar of Christ 34, 40
  Zelus Domus Dei 52
partition 99, 107, 147
  Iraq 110
passports 150
Paul, St 34, 40, 44
pax Romana 26
peace 54
  Christian 35, 37
  secular 54
Peace of Augsburg 50
Peace of Paris 2
Peace of Utrecht 51, 53
Peace of Westphalia 28, 50,
  51, 52
piracy 141
Poland 66–7, 100, 102
  partition 66–7
Portugal 69
  Portuguese Empire 69
prescription 62, 65
  ex injuria jus oritur 62
protestant sects and
  congregations 39
Protestantism 44
Prussia 28, 66

Quebec xiii 2, 4, 98, 103
  Parti Québecois 103
  secession 103

race 75
religious orders 32–33
Reformation 37, 42, 44, 45,
  50, 58
  Catholic Counter-
    Reformation 39

Renaissance 37, 42, 49, 50
respublica Christiana
    ('Christian
    Commonwealth') 26,
    27, 33–38, 40, 43, 44,
    45, 47, 51, 52, 57
Ritter, Gerhard 64
Roman Empire 7, 25, 36, 67m,
    152
Roman Law
    jus civile 7
    jus gentium 7
Roman Catholics 48
    emancipated 48
Romania 100
Roosevelt, Franklin Delano 3,
    16
Rousseau, Jean-Jacques 60,
    94–95
'rule of law' 85
Russia 66, 153
    Russian Revolution 96

Saudi Arabia 17
secession 99, 107, 111,
    147
Second World War 97, 99,
    102, 121, 125
    Nazi atrocities 121, 125
Seldon, John 65, 72
serfdom 117
Seven Years War 70
Skinner, Quentin 20
slavery 117
    Anti-Slavery Society 117
    emancipation 117
    household 117
    'virtual slavery' 117
social Darwinism 74
society of sovereign states 52,
    53, 76, 144–9
    conservative club 111–12
    global system x
Somalia 127
Soros, George 135

sovereignty
    citizenship 150–1
    cives 31
    civitas 31
    continuity 149, 160–1
    definition 10–11
    democratic 87–93
    dilemma of power 18–19
    discourse and language
        19–23, 159–160
    dynastic 61–66
    'end of history' 112–13
    evolution 112, 147–9
    idea ix, x, xii, 1, 6, 7, 8,
        12–13, 14, 23, 56
    imperial 56, 64, 72–7
    interdisciplinary studies xii
    international law 123
    meaning and usage x, xi,
        19–21
    parliamentary 56, 67, 83–7
    'the people' 30, 65, 78, 82,
        86, 88, 92, 105
    pluralistic reality 11, 49
    pooled 8, 148
    popular 56, 59–60, 61, 67,
        78–113
    post-sovereign world 139
    power and authority 14–18
    presuppositions 150–9
    racial 74–75
    responsibility 17–19
    self-determination 71–2, 76,
        77, 100, 106
    self-government 76
    slavery 117
    'sovereignty of social
        thought' 86
    terra nullius 72
    territorial 8–9, 72–3,
        104–112
    transfers of sovereignty
        76–77
Soviet Union 4, 102, 109,
    122

Spain 69
Spanish Empire 69
Spanish Armada 50
Stalin, Joseph 102
'state, the' 25, 30, 31, 61, 65, 97
  meaning and usage 4–5, 28
  Stato 38
  'unit of accountability' 138
statecraft 42
  art of government 42
  dynastic 64
  humanitarian 114–15
  raison d'état 42–3, 66
  realpolitik 68
Sweden 28
Reformation 45

Talleyrand, Charles Maurice de 65
Talmon, J.L. 94
terrorism 95, 135–8, 143, 155–9
  definition 159
  state-sponsored 158–9
  United Kingdom Terrorism Act 2000 156, 159
Thirty Years War 50, 52
totalitarian states 115
Truman, Harry 17

United Nations 4, 115
  Charter 8, 108, 120, 131
  General Assembly Resolutions 77
  General Assembly Declaration on the Granting of Independence 108
  Report of the High Level Panel on Threats, Challenges and Change 131
  Security Council 130, 131–2

Trusteeship Council 76
Universal Declaration of Human Rights 120
United States of America xiii, 17–18, 79, 82, 87, 88, 109–110
  the American people 79–82, 105
  American Revolution 79, 105
  Bill of Rights 79, 120
  Civil Rights Act 83
  Civil War 79
  Confederate States of America xiii, 3, 13, 80
  Congress 86–7
  Constitution 39, 79, 80, 93, 117
  'Declaration of Independence' xiii, 2, 79, 80
  desegregation and enfranchisement of African Americans 83
  extraterritorial jurisdiction 74
  Federalists 82
  First Amendment 39
  human rights protections 12
  'melting pot' 101
  Patriot Act of Congress 136
  quasi-imperial state 152–3
  September 11, 2001 135–6
  Supreme Court 83
  War of Independence 70, 80

Vattel, Emerich de 53
Von Mises, Ludwig 63

war 35–6
  just 35
  holy 35

war (cont.)
    medieval 41
    modern 41
War of the Spanish Succession
    51
Western (European) Empires
    66–72
Wight, M. 50
Wilson, Woodrow 3, 75, 99,
    100, 146, 153

world of sovereign states
    145–7

Yugoslavia 4, 102, 109,
    110–11
    civil war 111
    dissolution 111

Zwingli, Ulrich 44

CPSIA information can be obtained at www.ICGtesting.com
Printed in the USA
BVOW010029030713

324873BV00019B/296/P